03/15
28.00

BIRDSONG

Sebastian Faulks's

BIRDSONG

Stage version by Rachel Wagstaff

OBERON BOOKS
LONDON

First published in 2010 by Oberon Books Ltd
521 Caledonian Road, London N7 9RH
Tel: +44 (0) 20 7607 3637 / Fax: +44 (0) 20 7607 3629
e-mail: info@oberonbooks.com
www.oberonbooks.com

Reprinted with revisions in 2013, 2014

A catalogue record for this book is available from the British Library.

PB ISBN: 978-1-84943-068-5
E ISBN: 978-1-84943-931-2

Front Cover Artwork:
Design: Sam Charrington
Illustrations: Steve Rawlings
Photograph: Jack Ladenburg

Printed and bound by Marston Book Services Limited, Didcot.

Visit www.oberonbooks.com to read more about all our books and to buy them. You will also find features, author interviews and news of any author events, and you can sign up for e-newsletters so that you're always first to hear about our new releases.

to my mother and father,
to my brothers

With many thanks to

Duncan Abel, Sam Adamson, Gillon Aitken, Polly Baddeley, Antonia Bance, Becky Barber, Mike Bartlett, Jack Bradley, Saffron Burrows, Mrs Byford, Rose Cobbe, Beatrice Curnew, Meg Davis, Sebastian Faulks, Nick Frankfort, Toby Frow, Tony Green, Stewart Gregg, James Illman, Emily Jordan, Barnaby Kay, Duncan Macmillan, Charlie Miller, Tim Morrell, Trevor Nunn, Kate Pakenham, Tobias Round, Vera Schove, George Spender, Jack Tilbury, Natalie Tilbury, Katherine Thomson-Jones, Lesley Thorne, Simon Vinnicombe, Alastair Whatley, Anne-Marie Woodley, Jon Woodley, all the actors who have contributed, and to my family and friends.

This revised script was written for the Original Theatre Company

Birdsong was first produced at the Comedy Theatre, London on 18 September 2010 by Creative Management and Productions (CMP) Becky Barber Productions, Act Productions, with the following cast:

(In order of speaking)

STEPHEN WRAYSFORD, Ben Barnes

RENÉ AZAIRE / CAPTAIN GRAY, Nicholas Farrell

LISETTE AZAIRE / PROSTITUTE, Florence Hall

ISABELLE AZAIRE, Genevieve O'Reilly

BÉRARD / COLONEL BARCLAY, Iain Mitchell

LUCIEN LEBRUN / PRIVATE BRENNAN, Billy Carter

JEANNE FOURMENTIER, Zoë Waites

JACK FIREBRACE, Lee Ross

ARTHUR SHAW, Paul Hawkyard

PRIVATE EVANS, Owain Arthur

PRIVATE TIPPER / LIEUTENANT ELLIS, Gregg Lowe

PRIVATE ADAMS / MILITARY POLICEMAN / LIEUTENANT LEVI, Jack Hawkins

PRIVATE DOUGLAS / ORDERLY / GERMAN, James Staddon

PRIVATE COKER / GERMAN, Joe Coen

MARGUERITE / NURSE, Annabel Topham

Creative Team

Writer Rachel Wagstaff
Director Trevor Nunn
Producers CMP Becky Barber and Act
Designer John Napier
Costume Emma Williams
Lighting David Howe
Projection Jon Driscoll & Gemma Carrington
Music Steven Edis
Sound Fergus O'Hare
Casting Maggie Lunn

Original music composed by Steven Edis

A new version was written for The Original Theatre Company. It opened on 25 January 2013 at the Haymarket Theatre, Basingstoke. Produced by The Original Theatre Company and Birdsong Productions Ltd., with the following cast:

(In order of speaking)

ARTHUR SHAW / LAMM, Liam McCormick
JACK FIREBRACE, Tim Treloar
TIPPER / GRÉGOIRE / BARMAN, Charlie G Hawkins
EVANS / GERMAN SOLDIER / LEVI, Tim van Eyken
ADAMS / BÉRARD / COLONEL BARCLAY, Arthur Bostrom
BRENNAN / ORDERLY / MILITARY POLICEMAN, Joshua Higgott
TURNER / RENÉ AZAIRE / CAPTAIN GRAY, Malcolm James
STEPHEN WRAYSFORD, Jonathan Smith
ISABELLE AZAIRE, Sarah Jayne Dunn
LISETTE AZAIRE / PROSTITUTE, Polly Hughes
NURSE / JEANNE, Poppy Roe
MARGUERITE / GERMAN SOLDIER / BARMAID, Emily Stride

Creative Team

Writer Rachel Wagstaff
Director Alastair Whatley
Producers Anne-Marie Woodley, Jon Woodley and Alastair Whatley
Designer Victoria Spearing
Costume Ed Holland
Lighting Alex Wardle for Charcoalblue
Music Tim van Eyken
Sound Dominic Bilkey
DSM Lauren Barclay
Assistant Director Charlotte Peters
Movement Director Lucie Pankhurst
Fight Director Tim Klotz-Davenport
Dialect Coach Tim Charrington

This revised version was written for The Original Theatre Company. It opened on 12 February 2014 at the Devonshire Park Theatre, Eastbourne. Produced by The Original Theatre Company and Birdsong Productions Ltd., with the following cast:

(In order of speaking)

ARTHUR SHAW, Simon Lloyd
JACK FIREBRACE, Peter Duncan
TIPPER / GRÉGOIRE, Jonny Clarke
TURNER / RENÉ AZAIRE / CAPTAIN GRAY, Malcolm James
EVANS, Samuel Martin
STEPHEN WRAYSFORD, George Banks
ORDERLY / BÉRARD / COLONEL BARCLAY, James Staddon
ISABELLE AZAIRE, Carolin Stoltz
LISETTE AZAIRE, Selma Brook
NURSE / JEANNE, Elizabeth Croft
MARGUERITE, Lucy Grattan
MILITARY POLICEMAN / LEVI, Alastair Whatley

All other parts played by members of the company

Creative Team

Writer Rachel Wagstaff
Director Alastair Whatley
Producers Anne-Marie Woodley, Jon Woodley and Alastair Whatley
Designer Victoria Spearing
Original Costume Design Ed Holland
Lighting Alex Wardle for Charcoalblue
Music Tim van Eyken
Sound Dominic Bilkey
DSM Lauren Barclay
Assistant Director Charlotte Peters
Movement Director Lucie Pankhurst
Military Advisor Tony Green
Dialect Coach Tim Charrington
CSM Roger Richardson
TSM Gareth Moss
Wardrobe Mistress Sinead Francis

Characters

(Including suggested doubling)

STEPHEN WRAYSFORD

JACK FIREBRACE

ISABELLE AZAIRE

TURNER / AZAIRE / GRAY

BÉRARD / BARCLAY / CHAPLAIN / ORDERLY

LISETTE / PROSTITUTE

JEANNE FOURMENTIER / NURSE

ARTHUR SHAW

TIPPER / GRÉGOIRE / BARMAN

EVANS / LEVI

MARGUERITE

Other roles are played by members of the company.

This revised version was written for the Original Theatre Company and Birdsong Productions

Tour 2014

ACT ONE

SCENE ONE

The sound of heavy rain. Music.

An Estaminet behind the lines. SHAW, EVANS and TURNER appear, laughing, smoking, chatting.

JACK emerges from the tunnel. Exhausted. He wipes his face.

EVANS begins to play a jig. JACK goes over to join his sapper friends.

SHAW: Where you've been?

JACK: Thought I heard something, right above our tunnel, so I stayed down for a few hours, had a bit of a listen.

SHAW: Jack –

JACK: I know. But I couldn't hear anything. It was probably just shellfire.

SHAW: Aye. But if it had been the Boche-

JACK: Then we'd ask for cover. Get those infantry boys to do something at last, eh?

JACK signals for a drink. Sees that TIPPER has entered.

JACK: Speak of the Devil. You lost, son?

TIPPER: I'm looking for Mr Wraysford. I just got 'ere.

JACK: Never met him. Sorry, mate. Get the boy a drink.

TIPPER: But, d'you know where he is?

SHAW: *(Shrugs.)* We're the sappers.

TIPPER: Oh! The sewer rats?!

SHAW rises, angry.

JACK: It's all right; he's just a kid.

TIPPER: I'm eighteen.

JACK: Course you are, son. What's your name?

TIPPER: Michael Tipper.

JACK: And does your mother know you're 'ere?

TIPPER / JACK: She was the one wot sent me, daft cow!

A barmaid gives JACK a drink. He hands it to TIPPER.

JACK: Now get that down you, son.

TIPPER drinks, splutters.

JACK: We'll find him tomorrow, eh?

EVANS pats his knees, smiles at the woman. The sound of shellfire. TIPPER flinches. More shellfire.

TURNER: D'you hear that?

JACK: Still miles off.

JACK sees that TURNER is shaking. Beat.

JACK: Here, Turner, d'you hear wot Arthur said about Evans, this very morning?

EVANS: Here we go.

JACK: He said, Evans, Evans here weren't fit to associate with pigs. So I stuck up for him. I said, oh yes he is!

EVANS: Cheeky bugger!

JACK: Mind you, Arthur Shaw, he can hardly talk. His relatives work in business. The iron and steel business. That's right, his mother irons and his father steals.

The men laugh. Even TURNER.

SHAW: Give us a song, eh Jack?

JACK: Gawd. At least let me 'ave a drink!

SHAW signals to the woman to get JACK another drink.

SHAW: What'll we sing? Hands across the sea?

JACK: Hands across my bloody arse!

JACK sings, reluctantly at first.

JACK: *(Sings.)* At the club one evening Evans was telling all his pals
How much he hated girls despite their golden curls
"You wouldn't catch me with a girl, you bet your life", said

14

he
"Girls possess no charms for me,"
Then one chap there at Evans began to leer
Picked up his cane and said to him, "Come here…"

The rest (including TIPPER) join in for the chorus.

EVANS holds his hand out to the woman, who dances with him.

Hold your hand out naughty boy
Hold your hand out naughty boy
Last night in the pale moonlight I saw yer, I saw yer-
With a nice girl in the park, you were strolling full of joy –

A shell lands nearby. Then another shell lands.

SCENE TWO

The firestep. Night-time.

JACK, even more exhausted, sits, takes out paper and pencil.

JACK: *(Slowly at first, as he writes.)* April 23rd 1916…. Dear
Margaret. Thank you for the parcel. The Oxo cubes went
down a treat. The socks was just what I need. Funny to
think of you knitting away, all this time… They say we're
going to move at last. The big attack. Finish 'em off. I'll be
home soon enough. Give my love to the boy. *(JACK yawns.)*
Your loving husband, Jack.

SHAW appears with a bowl of water.

JACK: Where's Evans?

SHAW: Writing a saucy postcard to that girl from t'bar. Here,
letter for you –

JACK: Read it out, eh?

*SHAW retrieves a letter from his pocket, opens and then reads it as
JACK washes himself.*

SHAW: My dearest Jack. How are you keeping? All our
thoughts and prayers are with you. Your mother –

JACK / SHAW: Gawd bless 'er –

SHAW: Says to tell you she hopes you liked the cake... I'm sorry to have to tell you – I'm sorry to have to tell you...

JACK: Arthur?

SHAW: It's your boy. He's not so well. Diphtheria. They've taken him to t'hospital.

SHAW hands JACK the letter. JACK reads.

SHAW: ... He'll be in good hands.

JACK: I should be with him. D'you think they'll let me have leave?

SHAW: No harm in asking –

JACK: I'll find the Captain.

SHAW: He'll be asleep. Nothing you can do now. We'll talk to him in t'morning, eh?

EVANS enters, holding a letter he's writing.

EVANS: How d'you say 'I was the handsome Welsh one' in French?

JACK: *(Bad accent.)* Je suis...

SHAW: La...

JACK: La tres...grosse *(Imitates 'large' to SHAW.)* ... Welshy.

EVANS: *(Writing.)* ... Welshy. Thanks, boys. Oh, and the Captain wants one of us on sentry duty.

JACK: I'll do it.

SHAW: Don't be soft.

JACK: I'm all right.

SHAW: You been down the tunnel fifteen hour –

JACK: I'm all right. Honest.

SHAW: Jack –

JACK: You boys get some sleep, eh? Look after Turner.

JACK pats SHAW on the shoulder. SHAW picks up the bowl of water, leaves with EVANS.

JACK gets into sentry position.

JACK: *(Wearily.)* Dear God. Please look after my boy. He's done nothing wrong. Let us all die if you must, but keep him safe. Save my boy John. Save my boy John... Save my boy... John...

JACK slumps forward.

Lieutenant STEPHEN WRAYSFORD enters, walks past the sleeping JACK. He stops, turns back. He kicks JACK awake.

STEPHEN: Were you asleep?

JACK: I...

STEPHEN: Were you asleep?

JACK: Yes, sir.

STEPHEN: Lieutenant Wraysford. Come and see me at dawn. You were asleep on duty. You know the punishment.

STEPHEN leaves.

Beat. JACK lights a cigarette as focus switches to:

The officers' dug-out. A wooden table, a gramophone, two chairs.

The sound of a nightingale.

STEPHEN sketches. A woman appears. White blouse, red skirt. The memory of ISABELLE AZAIRE.

TIPPER enters with a rat on a bayonet. He looks disgusted. No response from STEPHEN. TIPPER coughs. STEPHEN looks up. The memory of ISABELLE disappears.

TIPPER: What do I do with this?

STEPHEN: Who are you?

TIPPER: Private Tipper, sir. You said if I saw any rats –

STEPHEN: Who?

TIPPER: I'm new. What do I do with the rat, Mr Wraysford?

STEPHEN: Bring it here.

TIPPER does so. STEPHEN pulls it off the bayonet, puts it on the table.

STEPHEN: Dismissed.

TIPPER leaves. STEPHEN goes over to the gramophone, turns it on. Music plays as STEPHEN goes back to the rat. STEPHEN takes out his knife, begins to dissect the rat.

Dawn approaches. JACK rises. Puts out his cigarette. Goes to STEPHEN.

Silence. JACK coughs.

STEPHEN: What d'you want?

JACK: You told me to report, sir.

STEPHEN: Did I?

JACK: I was asleep on duty.

STEPHEN: Well, you know the punishment.

JACK: Yes, sir. If I might –

STEPHEN: Shh – I'm reading the entrails.

Pause.

JACK: Sir, thing is, I'd been down in the tunnel all day –

STEPHEN silences the gramophone.

STEPHEN: You're one of the sappers?

JACK: Yes, sir.

STEPHEN: My men think you're wasting your time.

JACK: That's 'cos we get paid more. Sir.

STEPHEN: What do you actually do down there?

JACK: Dig.

STEPHEN: Yes, I got that.

JACK: … We dig about seventy foot down, as close as we can to the Boche, lay our mines beneath 'em, and when we're about to attack, we blow 'em all sky high, before your lot pour over –

STEPHEN: You dig towards the Boche.

JACK: Yes, sir.

STEPHEN: And they're digging towards us.

JACK: Yes. Sir, I'd be down there for fifteen hours, and then the boys and I were helping your lot, clear all the bodies where the trench was hit, and then I was put on sentry duty –

STEPHEN: You're digging towards the Boche, trying to find them, and they're digging towards you, trying to find us. Is that right?

JACK: That's about the size of it sir.

STEPHEN: So what happens if you meet in the middle?

Silence.

STEPHEN: What are they like, these tunnels of yours?

JACK: Like, sir? Like…tunnels.

STEPHEN: How big are they?

JACK: About three foot wide. Sometimes you can even stand.

STEPHEN: And you spend hours down there at a time.

JACK: 'bout ten, sir. Sometimes we sleep in 'em. Sir, last night –

STEPHEN: I'd like to see one.

JACK: No, sir. You wouldn't.

STEPHEN: I'd like to see what it's like.

JACK: Sir, about the charge –

STEPHEN: What charge?

JACK: You was going to court martial me. But I'd just got this letter, you see. About my son. He's not so well. Diptheria. He's only eight. He could be dying.

STEPHEN: Half the world's dying.

JACK: … Sir.

STEPHEN goes back to his rat.

JACK: When will it be?

STEPHEN: What?

JACK: The court martial.

STEPHEN: Why were you on sentry duty?

JACK: We do fatigues for you. When you're…running short.

STEPHEN: But you're a sapper. So you're not in my unit.

JACK: No.

STEPHEN: Well then. Dismissed.

Beat.

JACK: Oh, thank you, sir.

STEPHEN: I'll see you in that tunnel.

JACK emerges from the officers' quarters. The sound of birdsong. It is almost light. JACK breathes in deeply. He lights a cigarette, hands trembling.

STEPHEN rises. He puts on a record. Mendelssohn. A moment.

JACK takes a deep drag, exhales the smoke.

JACK: Thank you, God. Thank you.

SCENE THREE

The tunnel.

JACK, TIPPER, TURNER, SHAW, STEPHEN and EVANS crawl along.

TIPPER: You didn't say we'd have to crawl!

TURNER: Shh!

TIPPER: I don't like this.

TURNER: It's quite safe, Tipper. You'll be able to stand in a bit.

They come to the listening post where there is more room. They stand, brush themselves down.

STEPHEN: How far down are we now?

TURNER: 'bout sixty feet.

JACK: This is the listening post. We'll be through there, in the explosives chamber. Best be quiet. Might be a Boche tunnel above ours… Evans, you stay with them, eh?

JACK, SHAW and TURNER begin to crawl off.

EVANS: I'll teach you how to play Fritz.

STEPHEN: What's Fritz?

EVANS: It's this game I made up. About the German, in his tunnel. Here, Tipper, you'll like this. We try to guess who he is. So, I might say, his name's Hans, and before the war, he was a circus clown!

TIPPER: How long do we have to stay here?

EVANS: It'll go quick as a flash.

Beat.

EVANS: D'you know any jokes?

TIPPER: S'not fucking right. I'm infantry, not a bloody sewer rat.

STEPHEN: They do sentry duty for us.

TIPPER: Sentry duty's a piece of cake compared to this –

STEPHEN: All right, Tripper, that'll do –

TIPPER: Tipper, sir. My name's Tipper.

Beat.

TIPPER: What if the earth caves in?

STEPHEN: Don't be stupid.

TIPPER: What if we get trapped down here? We'd die of thirst, or we'd suffocate –

STEPHEN: Be quiet.

TIPPER: What if they blow it, and we can't get back? I think I'm going to be sick.

STEPHEN: Jesus Christ.

TIPPER vomits.

EVANS: Maybe you should send him back, Mr Wraysford –

STEPHEN: He'll go back when I say so!

TIPPER sobs loudly.

STEPHEN: Be quiet! Tipper, they'll hear you! D'you want to get us all killed?

TIPPER sobs on.

STEPHEN: I'll put you on a charge. Tipper… Be quiet! Right, I'm giving you till ten.

STEPHEN takes out his revolver, cocks it. TIPPER continues to cry loudly.

EVANS: Sir, you can't –

STEPHEN: One, two, three, four, five –

EVANS: Mr. Wraysford –

STEPHEN: Six, seven, eight –

An explosion. The men are thrown to the ground.

STEPHEN helps TIPPER and EVANS to their feet. TIPPER and STEPHEN stand in front of EVANS, guns raised.

STEPHEN: *(Whispers.)* All right, Tipper?

TIPPER nods.

STEPHEN: Grenade.

TIPPER takes out a grenade. Germans appear.

GERMAN 1: *(German.)* Halt!

STEPHEN: Hands up! Hands up!

A German fires his gun. EVANS is hit. STEPHEN takes out one German as he fires, and then is hit.

Meanwhile, TIPPER fumbles with the grenade. TIPPER throws the grenade. Explosion. The Germans fall to the ground.

JACK crawls in quickly.

JACK: Are there any more?

TIPPER: I don't know. I don't know! I killed them. I killed them!

JACK: All right. Calm down son. 'Ere. Take this –

JACK picks up and hands TIPPER a German Luger pistol.

JACK: Souvenir.

SHAW crawls in.

EVANS: Where's Turner?

SHAW: He's dead.

JACK: … Evans. You all right to get back?

EVANS: Course I bloody am. I'll get Turner.

JACK: We'll find him. Get that seen to. Tipper, give him an hand, eh?

TIPPER leaves, helping EVANS.

JACK: Sir, can you hear me? Mr. Wraysford?

Silence. STEPHEN is unconscious.

SHAW: Jack. He's bought it.

JACK: You take 'im back, I'll fetch Turner.

SHAW: There's nowt of Turner left.

JACK: … Shit.

SHAW: C'mon. Before the Boche come back.

SHAW turns to go.

JACK: No, give us an 'and.

SHAW: He's a goner.

JACK: He'll have family, won't he? Give them somewhere to come.

SCENE FOUR

Stretcher-bearers come through with a body on a stretcher. They dump it on a pile of bodies, leave.

The clearing station. Night-time. An ORDERLY stands with a clipboard. JACK goes to him.

JACK: This the clearing station?

ORDERLY: No, it's the bloody Savoy Hotel.

JACK: They told me a Lieutenant Wraysford had been taken here.

ORDERLY: Wraysford…? I'm sorry. They put him over the wall.

JACK: Right… Can I go and – I'd like to say a prayer for him.

ORDERLY: Whatever for?

JACK: He let me off a court martial.

ORDERLY: Down the muddy track. It's a ploughed field, grey stone wall. You can't miss it. Rows and rows of bodies. Stinks like hell.

The ORDERLY disappears.

A lone nightingale sings. JACK goes towards the bodies. He covers his nose, kneels to pray.

JACK: I pray for this man, Mr Wraysford, and for his life, such as it was.

Suddenly, from the darkness, a body moves in the pile.

JACK: Sir? It's me. Firebrace, sir. Stretcher! Stretcher-bearer! Come on, sir. You gotta 'ave something, someone worth living for.

Silence, bar the sound of the nightingale singing. Then music plays. ISABELLE AZAIRE runs on. And STEPHEN allows himself to remember...

SCENE FIVE

Music. A warm summer's evening, Amiens, 1910. The Azaires' garden. Wicker chairs, roses.

ISABELLE is joined by LISETTE. They spin each other round, laughing, dancing.

ISABELLE and LISETTE spin apart, ISABELLE directly in front of STEPHEN.

STEPHEN: Hello.

ISABELLE: Hello.

Beat.

ISABELLE: Are you the Englishman?

STEPHEN: Is it that obvious?

They smile.

LISETTE giggles.

ISABELLE: Lisette, fetch Papa –

Beat. LISETTE smiles at STEPHEN, runs off.

STEPHEN: I think your father's expecting me tomorrow, but –

ISABELLE: My father?

STEPHEN: You must be Monsieur Azaire's daughter...

ISABELLE: No. I'm his –

RENÉ AZAIRE appears, followed by MONSIEUR BÉRARD.

AZAIRE: Ah, Monsieur Wraysford! We weren't expecting you till tomorrow.

STEPHEN: I did send a telegram –

LISETTE and GRÉGOIRE run in.

AZAIRE: I told you not to run.

The children stand still immediately. Apprehensive. ISABELLE holds out her hand. They go to her.

AZAIRE: My son, Grégoire. My daughter, Lisette, and our neighbour, Municipal Councillor, and friend, Monsieur Bérard. Oh, and my wife.

STEPHEN looks at ISABELLE. A moment.

BÉRARD: How did you come here?

STEPHEN: By train.

BÉRARD: We're a great junction here – trains to Paris, to Lille, Boulogne... Of course the railways are very important to us because our country is five times the size of yours.

STEPHEN: ... I –

BÉRARD: Will you be staying for long?

STEPHEN: Perhaps a month. *(To AZAIRE.)* If that's all right –

AZAIRE: Of course, but –

BÉRARD: And the rain! It rains five days out of six in London, so I hear. Can you imagine, Madame?

STEPHEN: I believe that last year, it rained more in Paris than in London.

25

LISETTE laughs.

AZAIRE: Lisette! *(Glaring at LISETTE, then turning to STEPHEN.)* I'm afraid Lisette is yet to learn manners.

LISETTE: D'you run a factory in England?

STEPHEN: My guardian does.

GRÉGOIRE: Why d'you have a guardian?

AZAIRE: Grégoire!

STEPHEN: My parents died when I was a boy.

ISABELLE: … I'm very sorry, Monsieur.

STEPHEN: It was a long time ago.

AZAIRE: Bed-time, children.

GRÉGOIRE clings to ISABELLE.

LISETTE: Can't I stay up a bit longer?

AZAIRE: Bed. Both of you. Now.

LISETTE: Goodnight, Maman. Goodnight Papa. Goodnight… Monsieur.

GRÉGOIRE kisses ISABELLE, goes to leave.

AZAIRE: Grégoire?

GRÉGOIRE reluctantly kisses AZAIRE. Beat. The children leave.

BÉRARD: You'll be able to learn a great deal. René's brought in a whole host of modern machines –

STEPHEN: How are the workers adapting?

AZAIRE: They'll come round.

ISABELLE: *(Softly.)* Do they have any choice?

AZAIRE: Do forgive my wife. She finds all this talk about factories rather dull.

Beat.

BÉRARD: And Amiens itself! Have you seen much of the town?

STEPHEN: I only arrived this evening.

BÉRARD: What about our cathedral? Surely you caught sight of it from the train?

STEPHEN: I'm afraid I –

BÉRARD: And here on the Boulevard, we're just next to our famous watergardens. We shall have to take a trip. What else would you recommend our young guest do, dear Madame?

ISABELLE: I…

BÉRARD: You must be able to think of something.

AZAIRE: I'm afraid my wife is not what you might call imaginative.

ISABELLE: The River Somme is said to be very good for trout… Do you like fishing, Monsieur?

STEPHEN: Very much. My grandfather used to take me. We'd sit by the river for hours, with worms and bits of bread. I loved being there with him. It felt as if we were on the brink of something extraordinary.

Beat.

BÉRARD: And how did you pass this lovely day, dear Madame?

ISABELLE: I – I went for a walk by the river… I heard piano music coming from a house. It was beautiful. I wanted to stop and ask whoever was playing what it was called.

BÉRARD: What was the name of the tune you heard?

ISABELLE: I don't know.

BÉRARD: Well, was it Beethoven? Chopin? Lizst?

ISABELLE: I'd never heard it before.

BÉRARD: It was probably one of those awful German tunes.

STEPHEN: But, if you'll forgive me, Monsieur, German music can be –

BÉRARD: Now, I'm going to do something in which I risk playing the fool. I am going to sing. No, no, there's no point trying to dissuade me.

BÉRARD sits uncomfortably close to ISABELLE. He sings directly to her.

BÉRARD: *(Sings.)*

One day the young men came back from the war
The corn was high and our sweethearts waited
With our mothers and sons upon the seashore
Our boat brought us home as the tide abated.

STEPHEN claps. ISABELLE rises. BÉRARD takes a deep breath, carries on singing.

But we yearned for dear days long past, long past;
We longed for days long past.

Uncomfortable silence.

BÉRARD: Well, Madame. Does that not stir the heart?

AZAIRE: It is getting rather late.

BÉRARD: What intrigues me, Madame, is what you were doing wandering about town on your own?

ISABELLE: *(Lightly.)* Surely you don't expect me to sit at home all day, Monsieur?

BÉRARD: I'm sure that you have many friends to visit.

AZAIRE: Are you all right, my dear? You look a little flushed.

BÉRARD: Ah! A circulation problem, no doubt. A common ailment among the fairer sex.

AZAIRE: No. My wife is of a nervous temperament. She suffers from headaches. Perhaps you should go to bed, Isabelle. I'll look in on you later.

Beat.

ISABELLE: Goodnight, Monsieur Bérard. Monsieur Wraysford.

A moment. ISABELLE leaves.

BÉRARD: Same time tomorrow?

An owl hoots as night falls. Musical underscore as the scene fades and STEPHEN begins to make his way to bed.

The sound of a sharp thud, then a cry. Another thud, a louder cry. STEPHEN moves towards the sound of the cries. Then, much louder, another thud and another cry. STEPHEN takes a step forward. A floorboard creaks. STEPHEN steps back into the shadows, holds his breath.

A door opens, a narrow shaft of light falls onstage. The sobs are more audible, then stifled. AZAIRE appears in his dressing gown, holding a slipper.

AZAIRE: Is anyone there?

Silence. AZAIRE leaves. STEPHEN clenches his fists.

JACK appears.

JACK: ... You gotta 'ave something, someone worth living for.

SHAW has appeared with a stretcher. JACK and SHAW load STEPHEN onto the stretcher.

SHAW: What's he saying?

JACK listens closely.

JACK: Isabelle... Come on. One, two, three –

JACK and SHAW lift the stretcher.

A NURSE appears, with a bed.

NURSE: Put him there.

JACK and SHAW carry STEPHEN to the bed. The nurse tends to STEPHEN.

SHAW: Like bleedin' Lazarus, this one.

The sound of shelling nearby. SHAW flinches.

JACK: You all right?

SHAW: Dunno how much longer I can take this noise.

JACK: You been saying that for years.

Beat.

JACK: I'll ask when we can have another night off, eh? I'll even work on some new jokes.

SHAW: About bloody time!

SHAW grins. JACK and SHAW leave.

STEPHEN wakes.

NURSE: You're awake! I'll fetch the doctor –

STEPHEN: Nurse. Come here.

Beat. The NURSE steps closer.

NURSE: What did you want to –

STEPHEN: What's your name?

NURSE: We're not allowed to…

STEPHEN: Please.

NURSE: Mary.

STEPHEN: I'm alive, Mary. I'm alive.

NURSE: Yes.

STEPHEN: You don't understand. Six years ago, I –

But the NURSE has gone. ISABELLE enters furtively, carrying two baskets.

STEPHEN jumps up.

STEPHEN: Madame! Can I help you?

ISABELLE: I can manage. Thank you.

Before ISABELLE can leave:

STEPHEN: You have a beautiful house.

ISABELLE: Thank you.

ISABELLE turns to go.

STEPHEN: Have you ever been to England?

ISABELLE: I'm afraid not.

STEPHEN: I'm told it rains all the time.

ISABELLE: And your little country is five times smaller than ours.

They smile.

ISABELLE: Well, I must –

STEPHEN: Have you lived in Amiens for long?

ISABELLE: Since I was married.

STEPHEN: Where did you grow up?

ISABELLE: Rouen. It is famous for its cathedral.

STEPHEN: I'm from Lincolnshire. It's very flat.

A moment.

STEPHEN: Your husband had a meeting so I came back. I hope I am not intruding.

ISABELLE: Not at all, Monsieur, but I really must –

STEPHEN: I had a tour of the factory today. What d'you think?

Beat. ISABELLE is curious, despite herself. She looks at the picture STEPHEN is holding out.

ISABELLE: … You've captured it very well.

STEPHEN: Rows and rows of women at machines, men in flat caps, their faces, so…

ISABELLE: Desperate.

A moment.

STEPHEN: Madame, I… Last night, I heard…sounds –

ISABELLE: Please. Excuse me, Monsieur –

STEPHEN: I'm sorry. I just wanted to –

LISETTE runs on, holding a comb.

LISETTE: Maman, will you comb my hair? And then can we play Colin-Maillard?

ISABELLE: When Grégoire's back.

LISETTE: Stephen, will you play?

ISABELLE: I'm sure *Monsieur* has work to do.

LISETTE shakes out her hair. ISABELLE combs LISETTE's hair in gentle strokes.

STEPHEN: What's Colin-Maillard?

LISETTE: You've never played Colin-Maillard?

STEPHEN: Not as far as I know.

ISABELLE: Then you are a lucky man. My sister and I used to play it all the time. *(Smiling.)* I still have the bruises.

LISETTE: Do you like my hair, Monsieur?

STEPHEN: *(Looking at ISABELLE.)* It's very pretty.

A moment between STEPHEN and ISABELLE.

GRÉGOIRE runs in.

GRÉGOIRE: Maman! I thought you'd gone –

ISABELLE: I'm here.

LISETTE: We can play now!

ISABELLE: We haven't got a blindfold.

STEPHEN: … Here. You can use this.

STEPHEN takes off his tie.

STEPHEN: What do I do?

ISABELLE takes it. She puts it over STEPHEN's eyes.

LISETTE: And now we spin you.

LISETTE/GRÉGOIRE: *(As they spin STEPHEN.)* One, two, three –

LISETTE: And now you have to find us!

STEPHEN stretches out his hands. GRÉGOIRE runs around STEPHEN. STEPHEN nearly trips over him.

ISABELLE: Grégoire!

STEPHEN moves towards ISABELLE's voice. Laughter.

STEPHEN reaches out. Catches ISABELLE.

STEPHEN takes off the blindfold. He looks at ISABELLE.

A moment.

LISETTE: My turn!

ISABELLE: I think we had better stop –

LISETTE: But Maman –

ISABELLE: Your father will be home any minute. Come on, my darlings.

ISABELLE leads GRÉGOIRE and LISETTE away.

STEPHEN reties his tie as the memory begins to fade.

The birdsong turns into the sound of shelling.

STEPHEN looks over.

The sound of guns, louder than ever.

STEPHEN goes back to his hospital bed.

A young wounded soldier is carried across on a stretcher.

And STEPHEN slips towards another memory. The sound of shelling turns into the sound of the factory. The lights grow warmer and sounds even louder till STEPHEN can bear it no longer.

STEPHEN breaks away from the memory of the factory.

The sound of birdsong, the river flowing by.

Piano music plays – Mendelssohn's 'Lied ohne Worte Opus 19, no.6'.

ISABELLE walks by with her basket, wearing a headscarf. She stops by the sound of the music.

STEPHEN: Madame! What are you doing here?

ISABELLE: I – I was going for a walk.

STEPHEN: Is this the house with the music?

ISABELLE: Yes.

STEPHEN: It is beautiful.

Beat.

STEPHEN: May I – ? *(Indicates her basket.)*

ISABELLE: No. Thank you… Shouldn't you be at the factory?

STEPHEN: I needed some air. I don't like confined spaces.

Beat.

ISABELLE: Well, I should –

STEPHEN looks between ISABELLE and the house with the music. A man appears, hand raised to ISABELLE.

STEPHEN: Ah.

ISABELLE: Monsieur! It's not what you think.

STEPHEN: …

ISABELLE: The leader of the workers lives here. I bring them food. Some of them have five or six children.

STEPHEN: Does your husband know?

ISABELLE: No.

STEPHEN: …

ISABELLE: If you saw them, begging, rooting through bins…

STEPHEN: You're very brave.

ISABELLE: Monsieur –

STEPHEN: Stephen –

ISABELLE: … Stephen. Please…

STEPHEN: I won't tell him.

    Beat.

ISABELLE: Thank you.

STEPHEN: Can I help?

ISABELLE: No. Thank you.

STEPHEN: I could carry the food, or –

ISABELLE: If he found out, he would kill you.

STEPHEN: That doesn't stop you.

ISABELLE: *(Smiling.)* You're very stubborn, aren't you, Monsieur?

STEPHEN: So are you.

    They smile.

ISABELLE: I have the children. Excuse me –

STEPHEN: How can you be old enough to be their mother?

ISABELLE: René was married before. His first wife died.

STEPHEN: I don't understand how you can bear it.

ISABELLE: Monsieur –

STEPHEN: Every night, I hear…sounds –

ISABELLE: I know.

STEPHEN takes her hand.

STEPHEN: Is there anything I can do?

ISABELLE: Let go of my hand.

STEPHEN: Isabelle.

ISABELLE: Please.

Beat. STEPHEN presses ISABELLE's hand to his lips. A moment.

ISABELLE leaves.

The sound of the factory, louder and louder, which turns back into the sound of shelling.

JACK goes to STEPHEN. Back in hospital.

JACK: Captain Gray wants to see you. Sir. He says he's got you home leave.

STEPHEN: What?

JACK: He's just outside. I wondered if you could 'ave a word about leave for me. So I can see my son. You remember, sir, I told you –

STEPHEN: I'm not going home.

JACK: What about your sweetheart?

STEPHEN: Who?

JACK: Isabelle.

The memory of ISABELLE appears. She is crying. JEANNE appears. Goes to comfort her.

JACK: Sir? Can you help?

STEPHEN: Tell him. Tell him –

STEPHEN breaks off. Turns to ISABELLE.

STEPHEN: Can I help?

ISABELLE shakes her head. She whispers something to JEANNE.

ISABELLE: Excuse me.

ISABELLE leaves.

JEANNE: You must be Monsieur Wraysford. I'm Isabelle's sister. Jeanne.

STEPHEN: It's nice to meet you.

JEANNE: You speak very good French. For an Englishman.

STEPHEN: Is that a compliment?

JEANNE laughs. STEPHEN turns to go after ISABELLE.

JEANNE: I'm just passing through. I had to go to Albert today. My father wanted me to meet someone. A friend of his.

STEPHEN: …

JEANNE: I don't know what to do.

STEPHEN: …

JEANNE: My sister says you're going back to England soon.

STEPHEN: … Yes.

JEANNE: It is easier to tell a stranger the truth.

Pause.

STEPHEN: Your father wishes you to marry his friend.

JEANNE: I have to give my answer tomorrow.

STEPHEN: Do you like this man?

JEANNE: He is sixty-three years old and apparently he is very rich… He barely spoke to me.

STEPHEN: … What would your father say if you refused?

JEANNE: He would never allow me to marry anyone else.

STEPHEN: So you would be trapped, until…

JEANNE: My father dies.

Beat.

STEPHEN: I could tell your fortune, if you like.

JEANNE: You're very kind.

STEPHEN: You're her sister.

JEANNE: … Monsieur… ?

STEPHEN: Is that why she was crying? At the thought that you might end up like –

ISABELLE returns, having washed her face.

JEANNE: Monsieur was about to tell my fortune.

STEPHEN: *(He takes out a pack of cards.)* When's your birthday, ma'amselle?

JEANNE: April 4th.

STEPHEN: You're looking for even numbers, red suits.

STEPHEN deals five cards. He turns them over one by one.

STEPHEN: Six of hearts…good…two of diamonds…yes…four of clubs…not bad… Jack of diamonds…and…the Queen of hearts.

JEANNE: What does that mean?

STEPHEN: You'll be very happy. As long as you have nothing to do with priests, or bearded women.

They laugh.

STEPHEN: It means that one day you'll marry a handsome stranger…and you'll be happy.

JEANNE: You cheated.

STEPHEN: I assure you –

JEANNE: You must have done.

STEPHEN: Why should I do that?

Beat.

ISABELLE: Tell mine.

Beat.

STEPHEN: When's your birthday?

ISABELLE: 17th December.

STEPHEN: You're looking for black suits. Odd numbers.

STEPHEN shuffles, then begins to deal the cards –

AZAIRE enters.

AZAIRE: Ma'amselle Jeanne. Isabelle didn't mention you were coming. Are you intending to stay with us for long?

JEANNE: I'm afraid I have to continue my journey home tonight.

AZAIRE: What a shame. Isabelle, we're going to the watergardens on Sunday. Ask Marguerite to prepare a picnic.

Silence.

AZAIRE: Would you like me to order you a carriage to the station?

JEANNE: I'm quite happy to walk.

AZAIRE: As you wish. Well then.

AZAIRE turns to go, expecting ISABELLE to follow.

AZAIRE: Isabelle.

ISABELLE and JEANNE embrace, cling to each other.

AZAIRE: Isabelle!

Beat. ISABELLE leaves. Silence.

JEANNE: Well, I should –

STEPHEN: You could run away.

JEANNE: Where to?

STEPHEN: I don't know. Paris!

JEANNE: And what would I do in Paris, Monsieur?

STEPHEN: You could work in a in a café!

JEANNE: Or set up my easel by the Seine and draw pictures for English tourists.

They smile. MARGUERITE appears, with JEANNE's summer coat. She hands them to JEANNE.

MARGUERITE: Ma'mselle Jeanne.

Beat.

JEANNE follows MARGUERITE out. Turns back to STEPHEN.

JEANNE: Thank you for your advice. I only wish it could come true.

STEPHEN: It will. If you let it.

Beat.

JEANNE: I wonder if we will ever meet again?

STEPHEN: I expect not... You will be all right.

JEANNE: I know.

JEANNE leaves.

JACK re-appears.

JACK: Sir. About my leave, sir. If you could have a word –

STEPHEN: What leave?

JACK: I just want to see my boy. One last time.

STEPHEN: ... I'll tell your fortune.

JACK: Sir?

STEPHEN: You're looking for black suits. Odd numbers.

STEPHEN begins to turn over the cards.

STEPHEN: Two of spades. Seven of clubs. Jack of diamonds. King of spades.

JACK: What does that mean?

STEPHEN: It means you'll be all right... As long as you avoid long dark places.

JACK chuckles.

STEPHEN: Tell Captain Gray to come in.

JACK: I'll give you a minute to, er, smarten yourself up. Sir.

As STEPHEN does indeed smarten himself up, JACK turns to a new page in his notepad.

JACK: Dear Margaret. Thank you for your letter. It is a great comfort for me to know that you are with our boy, and that they are looking after him in the hospital. I keep asking for leave but I haven't had much luck yet. Margaret, I... I wanted to tell you. I prayed for this officer and he made it, even though he was a goner. I pray for John too, night and day, so he'll make it too, won't he? And then I'll come back to you. I'll come back to you both, I swear.

Captain GRAY appears. JACK leaves.

GRAY: Wraysford.

STEPHEN: Captain Gray. What's all this nonsense about leave?

GRAY: What?

STEPHEN: We're about to move.

GRAY: That's as may be, but those are my orders. Two weeks' home leave. Well. That's all, Wraysford.

GRAY turns to leave.

STEPHEN: No thank you. Sir.

GRAY: *(Turning back.)* I beg your pardon?

STEPHEN: I don't need leave.

GRAY: Don't be ridiculous! They gave you up for dead three weeks ago. You need rest.

STEPHEN: I can't abandon my men.

GRAY: They depend on you?

STEPHEN: They obey me.

GRAY: Do you think that's enough?

STEPHEN: Probably.

GRAY: You've got to make them like you, Wraysford. That's the secret… No one wants to die fighting for some stuffed shirt.

STEPHEN: I set an example.

GRAY: I'm sure you do. Would you give up your own life for them?

STEPHEN: … No.

GRAY: Because you value your life more than the life of a simple footsoldier. You have to love them, Wraysford.

Beat.

STEPHEN: Is it true we're moving to Amiens?

GRAY: I'm sorry, Wraysford.

STEPHEN: I used to live there. I know the whole area.

GRAY: I'm sure it's changed a great deal since then. Go home, Wraysford.

STEPHEN: A sapper wanted me to ask you about leave on his behalf. Why not send him home instead?

GRAY: We'll need every one of the sappers to lay the mines when we go over. Look, I'm offering you a ticket home. I've got men, shooting themselves in the foot to get back. Why will you not go home?

STEPHEN: This is my home.

GRAY: You must have some family, friends, a sweetheart...

Silence.

STEPHEN: You told me to love my men. I can't help them from a café in London.

GRAY smiles.

STEPHEN: I want to finish what we started. I need to understand.

GRAY: Understand what?

STEPHEN: Why I was brought back, right here. What all this is for. The fighting and the killing, and the trenches, and the tunnels, and the rats and the lice. How far we can go and still call ourselves human. How many more will die before it's enough? Five million? Eight million? Ten million? I have to try to understand. If you send me away now, then I've got no chance. Something happened to me, here, in France, six years ago and, since then. If I can understand this war... Sir, please. This is my only chance.

Beat.

You promoted me. You brought me here. Surely I must have some use.

Beat.

STEPHEN: Where are we moving to?

GRAY: Albert, near the River Somme.

STEPHEN: The Somme? I've been there.

ISABELLE appears.

GRAY: Wraysford?

STEPHEN: We had a…

The sound of the watergardens. MARGUERITE lays a picnic blanket. LISETTE, GRÉGOIRE and ISABELLE spread a picnic. GRÉGOIRE winds up a small gramophone.

Sunday. The watergardens: a hot day in early July, 1910.

BÉRARD stands gesticulating. ISABELLE and STEPHEN stare at each other. Music plays.

BÉRARD: And as you can see, the watergardens are formed by the backwaters of the Somme… Man and nature working in perfect harmony… And if you look to your left, you'll see some plots of land…

BÉRARD mops his forehead with his handkerchief. LISETTE and MARGUERITE pay BÉRARD polite attention. GRÉGOIRE yawns. MARGUERITE shushes GRÉGOIRE.

MARGUERITE: Monsieur? A drink.

MARGUERITE pours BÉRARD a drink.

STEPHEN: *(Quietly.)* May I draw you?

ISABELLE: With what?

STEPHEN takes a small notepad from his pocket.

STEPHEN: With your permission… Madame.

ISABELLE: *(Smiling.)* … You did not ask before.

STEPHEN goes to ISABELLE. A moment. STEPHEN begins to draw ISABELLE.

BÉRARD: Owned by farmers, who live in the town.

The music builds as STEPHEN moves closer to ISABELLE.

BÉRARD: Generations of fathers and sons, handing it on to their offspring, as it has been passed to them in their turn, by all those who have gone before. It is rather moving, is it not Madame?

STEPHEN is drawn closer yet as the music builds to a crescendo.

GRÉGOIRE knocks over the gramophone.

MARGUERITE: Grégoire!

BÉRARD: I said, Madame, do you not find it stirring that everything always continues here untouched. As it has for generations.

STEPHEN and ISABELLE spring apart.

STEPHEN puts his notepad away. He takes out a wooden carving and his knife.

GRÉGOIRE: What's that?

STEPHEN: Just a carving.

LISETTE: She's so pretty! Can I have it?

STEPHEN: … Of course.

STEPHEN hands it to her.

GRÉGOIRE: Can I see your knife?

STEPHEN: Yes. But be careful. Don't touch the blade.

STEPHEN hands GRÉGOIRE his knife. LISETTE and GRÉGOIRE look at each other. Both triumphant.

AZAIRE rushes on.

BÉRARD: Ah! There you are.

AZAIRE: We have to leave. My workers want to strike. I must speak to the police.

ISABELLE's eyes seek out STEPHEN's.

BÉRARD: I can escort your wife home.

AZAIRE: Why don't you come with me? Isn't the police commissioner a friend of yours? You could tell him to arm his men. Some bloodshed might be no bad thing.

STEPHEN: I can accompany your wife and children home.

AZAIRE: Thank you. Well then –

Beat. BÉRARD follows AZAIRE off.

ISABELLE: … Children. Help Marguerite to pack up.

They begin to pack up the picnic. STEPHEN goes to ISABELLE quickly.

ISABELLE: Monsieur. I…

STEPHEN: Anything.

ISABELLE: Do you remember how to find the house –

STEPHEN: With the music. Of course.

ISABELLE: The police won't care if someone is hurt, or killed –

STEPHEN: I'll go tonight. I'll make sure your friend knows.

ISABELLE: Thank you, Monsieur.

STEPHEN: Stephen.

ISABELLE: … You are very kind.

STEPHEN: I'd do anything for you. Do you understand?

ISABELLE leaves.

GRÉGOIRE: Monsieur!

GRÉGOIRE runs to give STEPHEN his knife back.

The scene fades as GRAY reappears.

GRAY: Tell me about the area.

STEPHEN: Open fields, heavily farmed. The banks of the River Somme are pretty marshy, and there's a long ridge on our side of it. The ground rises steeply up to a hamlet called Thiepval… To attack up that hill would be suicide.

GRAY: The Germans have been there almost two years. I don't suppose they'll have chosen the lower ground.

STEPHEN: Who's going?

GRAY: Kitchener's Army.

STEPHEN: The new boys?

GRAY: With a few regulars to stiffen them up.

STEPHEN: The office boys? The clerks? The farm hands?

GRAY: I'd thoroughly recommend Norfolk at this time of year.

STEPHEN: No. Thank you, sir.

GRAY: All right. On one condition. You have to stop all the nonsense.

STEPHEN: What nonsense?

GRAY: I've seen that rubbish in your dug-out. The rats and reading the cards… Officers aren't superstitious, Wraysford.

STEPHEN: It's just a game, sir.

GRAY: I don't know your life history but children need to believe in powers outside themselves. That's why they read books about witches and wizards and God knows what. There is a human need for that kind of thing which childhood normally exhausts. But if a child's world is broken up too early –

STEPHEN: What ridiculous Austrian quack –

GRAY: If you keep doing that nonsense, you'll die! Look, I understand you need a, a distraction but can you not find some other way?

STEPHEN: Sir?

GRAY: I'm told there's a peasant woman and her daughter in Auchonvillers who can work their way through an entire battalion in a week… Remarkable people, the French.

STEPHEN: … !

GRAY: Get some rest, man. You look a bloody mess.

GRAY leaves. The scene disappears, replaced by the sound of the factory. The sound of workers cheering, then doors opening, and gunshots. Screams, confusion, fear.

SCENE SIX

The Azaires' drawing room. ISABELLE is combing LISETTE's hair.

STEPHEN looks down at his hand. It is bleeding.

LISETTE: What happened to your hand?

STEPHEN: I got it caught.

LISETTE: Let me see –

ISABELLE: Lisette, fetch Marguerite to bandage Monsieur's hand.

LISETTE: Can't I do it?

STEPHEN: Thank you.

Beat. LISETTE leaves.

ISABELLE: Stephen –

STEPHEN: I gave him the message. They were ready.

ISABELLE: Was anyone hurt?

STEPHEN: No.

ISABELLE: … Thank you.

STEPHEN: Isabelle –

ISABELLE: What happened to your hand?

STEPHEN: I hit one of the workers.

ISABELLE: Why?

STEPHEN: He…insulted…someone.

ISABELLE: What did he say?

STEPHEN: It doesn't matter.

ISABELLE: Monsieur.

STEPHEN: He implied something about your friendship with the worker you take food to.

ISABELLE: But I only –

STEPHEN: I know.

LISETTE comes in with a bowl and cloth.

LISETTE: Hold out your hand… It might sting a bit.

LISETTE gently cleans STEPHEN's hand.

STEPHEN: Madame, there's been a little trouble at the factory. Your husband wishes me to work here, until things calm down... It should only be for a few days. Is that all right?

ISABELLE: Of course.

LISETTE: You could help me with my homework! I've got to learn lots of English words. And Françoise, my best friend, she really wants to meet you.

STEPHEN: Françoise? That's a pretty name.

LISETTE: She's really ugly.

MARGUERITE enters with a telegram.

MARGUERITE: A telegram, Monsieur.

MARGUERITE hands STEPHEN a telegram, leaves. STEPHEN reads it.

Pause.

STEPHEN: My guardian wants me back in England.

LISETTE: But you can't go! We're going to Auchonvillers on Sunday... You could fish in the river, and we'd take a horse and trap... At least stay till then.

STEPHEN: I'll see what I can do.

LISETTE: Please, Monsieur –

ISABELLE: He said he'd try.

LISETTE desperately tries not to cry.

ISABELLE: Lisette? Are you all right?

LISETTE: Yes. Just a little tired.

STEPHEN: Perhaps you should go to bed.

LISETTE: Monsieur?

STEPHEN: And then, if you are feeling better later, I could help you with your homework.

Pause.

LISETTE: Maman, is it all right if I go to my room?

ISABELLE: Of course.

LISETTE: … Monsieur.

LISETTE leaves.

ISABELLE: Would you like some coffee?

STEPHEN: …

ISABELLE: Or tea. I know you English prefer tea.

STEPHEN: No.

ISABELLE: I could ask Marguerite to order you a carriage to the station, Monsieur.

STEPHEN: Stephen. My name is Stephen.

ISABELLE: …

STEPHEN: Tell me you feel nothing for me, and I'll go.

ISABELLE: … I'm very grateful for what you have done for the workers –

STEPHEN: For you.

ISABELLE: You're so young.

STEPHEN: So are you.

ISABELLE: You're my husband's guest.

STEPHEN: So?

ISABELLE: You have to go.

STEPHEN: D'you love him?

ISABELLE: He's my husband.

STEPHEN: Do you love him?

ISABELLE: You're just a boy, passing through –

STEPHEN: No –

ISABELLE: But this is my home. Do you understand?

STEPHEN: I –

ISABELLE: I don't want to be pitied!

STEPHEN: I want to kiss you.

ISABELLE: …

STEPHEN: Do you have any idea how beautiful you are?

Pause.

ISABELLE: And then you'll go back to England.

STEPHEN: I'll write to my guardian. I'll tell him I'm not going home –

ISABELLE: Don't be silly –

STEPHEN: I love you.

STEPHEN goes to her. She pulls away.

ISABELLE: I hardly – it's not right.

STEPHEN: You hardly what?

ISABELLE: I'm married.

STEPHEN: To a man who beats you… How can someone so brave be such a coward?

ISABELLE: …

STEPHEN: I love you. I always will.

STEPHEN lays the back of his hand against her cheek.

They kiss. ISABELLE pulls away.

ISABELLE: Come to the red room.

ISABELLE walks away.

TIPPER appears. 1916. Back in hospital. STEPHEN is caught between times.

TIPPER: I came to say goodbye, sir.

STEPHEN: What?

TIPPER: We're about to move.

EVANS appears. Plays music: the Mendelssohn.

Birdsong. A red light illuminates Isabelle. The red room. TIPPER leaves.

The music builds. STEPHEN goes to her. They kiss passionately.

They make love.

They curl up together.

ISABELLE gets up, leaves and the music fades. She is replaced by the nurse, holding an army blanket.

NURSE: Lieutenant Wraysford?

STEPHEN looks round. The bed is now the hospital bed.

STEPHEN: I have to get back to Amiens.

NURSE: But Captain Gray said –

STEPHEN: Tell him, tell him I'll see him at the Somme.

SCENE SEVEN

EVANS sings the first two lines of 'Mademoiselle from Armentières'. He jumps on SHAW's back.

SHAW: Get off!

EVANS: You all right, Arthur?

SHAW: How d'you do it?

EVANS: What?

SHAW: Keep larking about.

EVANS: Well, we're still here, aren't we? Hey, Tipper! D'you want to play Fritz?

TIPPER has joined them, with a couple of infantry men.

TIPPER: I hate that stupid game!

EVANS: What's wrong with it?

TIPPER: Well, what's it for?

EVANS: Keeps you safe, boyo.

TIPPER: How?

JACK has joined them.

JACK: The Hun can't get you if you can see him first.

TIPPER: … Go on then. How d'you play again?

EVANS: Well, I might say, there's this fellow, bandy knees but an enormous –

STEPHEN appears.

JACK: Attention!

TIPPER: Bloody hell!

STEPHEN: It's all right, Tipper. I'm not Jesus.

TIPPER laughs.

EVANS: Well done, sir.

STEPHEN: What?

EVANS: You made a joke.

STEPHEN: Did I? Yes, I suppose I did. Well then. Fall in. Off we go.

The men begin to march, singing: 'Take Me Back to Dear Old Blighty'.

They stop singing, slow down, stare to one side.

STEPHEN: Is there a problem?

TIPPER: What's that, sir?

STEPHEN: A grave…a mass grave.

TIPPER: For us?

The sound of birdsong; this turns into the sound of howitzers, shelling.

STEPHEN: Nearly there, boys.

TIPPER: Where's there?

STEPHEN: Auchonvillers.

A girl appears. ISABELLE?

STEPHEN: You can have the night off. Dismissed.

The men leave.

STEPHEN goes to the girl. A red light falls on the stage, illuminating a bed.

PROSTITUTE: Monsieur! Would you like to –

STEPHEN: I – I was looking for someone. Excuse me.

PROSTITUTE: Monsieur? Are you sure you wouldn't like to –

STEPHEN: No. Thank you.

PROSTITUTE: Am I not pretty enough?

Beat.

STEPHEN: How much?

PROSTITUTE: Five francs.

STEPHEN goes to the PROSTITUTE.

ISABELLE appears in the shadows.

The sound of birds. Early afternoon. The red room. The clock chimes – five o'clock.

STEPHEN: Let me see you.

ISABELLE hides under the blanket. STEPHEN pulls the blanket off her. ISABELLE laughs.

STEPHEN: You have a beautiful smile.

ISABELLE: You have a beautiful stare!

STEPHEN: I don't stare! Come away with me.

ISABELLE: Tell me something about your life. About your family.

STEPHEN: My father left before I was born. My mother died when I was four.

ISABELLE: Do you remember her?

STEPHEN: Just her voice. I was brought up by my grandfather. Then I was sent to an orphanage. Then I was rescued by my guardian. Come away with me.

ISABELLE: Why were you sent to an orphanage?

STEPHEN: Well, one day, when I was ten, I came home from school and my grandfather was gone. There was just a strange man, waiting for me.

ISABELLE: What had happened?

Beat.

ISABELLE: I have to understand you.

STEPHEN: This man said that my grandfather had been sent to prison.

ISABELLE: Why?

STEPHEN: I don't know. They never told me what he was meant to have done. I went to the orphanage but I didn't stay long. There was a dead crow, nailed to a fence. It was crawling with maggots – sorry! A boy dared me to stroke it but I wouldn't, so he laughed at me, so I hit him and – they wrote about us in the local papers. The man who became my guardian read about it, and he rescued me.

ISABELLE: I wish I could have rescued you.

STEPHEN: You would have been…what…

ISABELLE: Seventeen.

They laugh.

STEPHEN: *(Teasing.)* You're so old!

ISABELLE: You're so young!

STEPHEN: Come away with me.

ISABELLE: Where would we go?

STEPHEN: Anywhere you like.

ISABELLE: How would we live?

STEPHEN: Does it matter? When I first saw you, I thought you were beautiful, but – no, listen. You were so alive. But here, in this house… We could go anywhere you like…

ISABELLE: I would disgrace my whole family. My father –

STEPHEN: What do you want?

ISABELLE: … I want… I want us always to come home to each other.

The bell chimes again for the half. ISABELLE grabs her clothes.

STEPHEN: I only have a few more days. Come with me.

ISABELLE: I –

They hear a noise, spring apart.

Then the sound of a pigeon.

ISABELLE: It's just a pigeon!

STEPHEN: Get rid of it!

ISABELLE: *(Laughing.)* It's just a little bird.

STEPHEN: Get rid of it. Please.

> *ISABELLE claps her hands. The sound of the bird flying off. ISABELLE goes to STEPHEN.*

ISABELLE: So there is something that frightens you.

> *The sound of the front door opening.*

ISABELLE: Quick –

STEPHEN: We only have one chance. One life. I'll work something out.

ISABELLE: I love you. I always will.

> *ISABELLE disappears.*

> *The PROSTITUTE goes over to a bowl of water. She kneels down, cups her hands together, washes herself between the legs.*

PROSTITUTE: Monsieur?

STEPHEN: She lied.

PROSTITUTE: Who did?

STEPHEN: Why d'you do this?

PROSTITUTE: My father was killed in the war. I need the money.

STEPHEN: Don't you care, about any of this? What you've seen, what we've done. Bodies, abandoned to rot, just forgotten; She promised me –

PROSTITUTE: I'm not her, Monsieur –

> *STEPHEN takes out his knife, opens the blade. The girl screams.*

STEPHEN: Why? Why would you do this?

PROSTITUTE: Please… Please… It's not my fault!

> *STEPHEN runs the knife down the girl's body. He brings the knife to her neck, rests it at her throat.*

> *Beat.*

> *STEPHEN drops the knife.*

> *The girl picks up the knife, closes the blade.*

STEPHEN: I'm sorry. I'm so sorry.

Beat.

The girl gives STEPHEN back his knife.

PROSTITUTE: It makes us animals. The war.

STEPHEN: The last time I was here –

ISABELLE appears. STEPHEN turns back to the girl, but she has gone.

A golden afternoon: Auchonvillers. The sound of the river. Birdsong. Picnickers.

STEPHEN rushes to ISABELLE.

STEPHEN: I've worked it all out. I've found a small house in Saint-Rémy, and I'll get a job, as a carpenter –

ISABELLE: What about the children? I can't just abandon them.

STEPHEN: Lisette's practically grown up. She'll marry soon and then…

ISABELLE: And Grégoire?

STEPHEN: … *(Gently.)* He isn't your child.

ISABELLE: … You could get a room, in Amiens –

STEPHEN: It wouldn't work. You know that. Come with me –

The sound of BÉRARD, humming. They dis-engage at once.

BÉRARD appears with a fishing rod.

BÉRARD: Ah, there you are, Madame! Are you feeling any better?

ISABELLE: Yes. I just needed a little walk.

BÉRARD: I was most concerned about you. Wandering off like that.

STEPHEN: Are you, er, enjoying the fishing, Monsieur?

BÉRARD: Very much. I have caught a large trout. I am very good at catching my prey.

A moment.

BÉRARD: Perhaps you should take a nice walk. If you head towards Thiepval, you'll see the most delightful countryside. Yes, if I were you, I'd take a nice long walk. Perhaps your last chance, eh, before you go back to England? Although I should warn you, it's all uphill.

Beat.

BÉRARD: Madame. Allow me to escort you to lunch.

ISABELLE leaves with BÉRARD.

STEPHEN sits down again.

LISETTE enters, puts her hand on his shoulder. STEPHEN takes the hand, strokes it. He spins around.

LISETTE: You thought I was someone else.

STEPHEN: What?

LISETTE: You thought I was her.

STEPHEN: I don't know what you mean.

LISETTE: *(Imitating lovemaking.)* Stephen… Isabelle!

STEPHEN: You have a very strong imagination.

LISETTE: I saw you, just now! I thought you liked me.

STEPHEN: I do like you. Just…

LISETTE: Am I not pretty enough?

STEPHEN: You're very pretty.

LISETTE: No one ever looks at me when I'm standing next to her.

STEPHEN: You're very pretty, Lisette.

LISETTE: Will you kiss me?

STEPHEN: I can't.

LISETTE: I'll tell my father.

STEPHEN: No!

LISETTE: …

STEPHEN: I know what it's like to have no mother.

LISETTE: So?

STEPHEN: Do you want to lose Isabelle too?

LISETTE: Every time I close my eyes, all I see is you.

STEPHEN: ...

LISETTE: If you make her abandon us, she'll never forgive
you.

STEPHEN: Lisette –

LISETTE: I'll tell him. I'll tell my father.

Pause.

STEPHEN: I'll kiss you. Just once. If you swear you won't say
anything, to anyone.

Pause. LISETTE nods.

STEPHEN kisses her.

LISETTE takes STEPHEN's hand, places it on her breasts.

Beat.

STEPHEN pulls his hand away.

LISETTE bursts into tears, throws the carving down. She runs off.

*The sound of the artillery. COLONEL BARCLAY appears, with his
sword – not the blimp-like figure the men expect but a hardened
professional soldier.*

GRAY: Company... Attention!

COLONEL BARCLAY: Gentlemen. I'm sure you all know why
we are here, in the valley of the River Somme. Tomorrow,
we shall inflict a defeat on the Boche such that he will
never recover...

Listen!

The artillery gets louder.

COLONEL BARCLAY: That is the sound of our artillery. As you
know, we've just dished out a *six-day* bombardment that'll
have cut every bit of German wire from here to Dar-es-
Salaam. If there's any Boche left alive, he'll be so relieved
it's all over, he'll come out with his hands in the air. But

that's not all. Our sapper friends have also been busy. Before we pour over, they will detonate their mines and blow the enemy sky-high.

The MEN cheer.

You will face men desperate to surrender. But we never can and never will surrender. Fight for the men who bore these colours before you. For the man fighting beside you. For your families. For your King. For your country. God bless you all...and we will meet again, tomorrow night.

GRAY: *(Quickly.)* Three Cheers for the Colonel. Hip hip –

MEN: *(Quickly.)* Hooray.

GRAY: *(Quickly.)* Hip hip –

MEN: *(Quickly.)* Hooray.

GRAY: *(Quickly.)* Hip hip –

MEN: *(Quickly.)* Hooray.

MILITARY POLICEMAN: All ranks are reminded that maintenance of good order and discipline in the coming operation is paramount. Those found straggling after their unit has advanced will be expected to account for themselves. If they fail to do so, they will also be subject to the full extent of military discipline. That's all. Company dismissed.

SHAW and JACK go back to the tunnel entrance.

JACK: Thank gawd we got a navy.

Beat.

JACK: Where's Evans?

SHAW: Went to see that prostitute in town. Randy bastard, that one. I'm bloody starving.

JACK: Saved you some fruitcake.

JACK gives SHAW the last of his fruitcake.

SHAW: Any news?

JACK: Post hasn't come yet.

SHAW: Good hospitals, back home.

JACK: Yeah.

SHAW: Your lad any good at football?

JACK: I'm trying to teach him. He loves it. He's not very big, so they always stick him in goal.

SHAW: He'll get better, when he's growed… Our lads can play together when we're done.

Beat.

JACK: I've been trying to draw him, but I can't get the face right…

SHAW: Let's see.

JACK hands over his notepad.

SHAW: He's got your nose, and chin.

JACK: Poor bugger… Arthur. Can I draw your picture sometime?

SHAW: … Yes.

EVANS enters, exhausted, rearranging his groin.

EVANS: Well, bugger me backwards! I am spent! And I had to wait in line for an hour and a half!

JACK: Well, at least the bloke behind you didn't have to wait too long.

EVANS: … Got any cigarettes?

JACK: I only got two left.

EVANS: I'll do you a trade.

EVANS holds out a letter, waves it around.

EVANS: Cigarette for this letter.

SHAW: Evans –

EVANS: I still haven't heard back from the French girl. So I've been thinking, maybe you told me the wrong thing to write…

SHAW: Give him his letter.

EVANS: Trade or nothing.

SHAW: Evans! Just give it him.

JACK: S'all right. Here.

JACK hands EVANS a cigarette. EVANS hands over the letter. EVANS lights his cigarette, goes off whistling.

SHAW: You didn't have to –

JACK: Leave it.

Pause.

SHAW: Open it, Jack.

JACK: In a bit.

SHAW: D'you want me to leave you be?

JACK: ... When we're digging the tube line back home, I'd think to myself I was in a railway carriage, the windows open, the wind in me face, this whole world of sky, and trees, and fields, just whistling by, only I couldn't see it, 'cos the shutters were down... But out here, in the tunnels, I can't even... I can't...

SHAW: Best to know.

Beat.

JACK: You read it to me, Arthur.

JACK hands him the letter.

SHAW reads aloud:

SHAW: My dearest Jack. How are you? Thank you for your letters, which have been a great comfort. I have to tell you that our boy – our boy died, this morning...

JACK: Go on.

Beat.

SHAW: The doctors said he suffered no pain. I am sorry to have to tell you this, my dear Jack, but you must not let it get you downhearted. You are all I have left now and I pray God will send you home to me... I'm to collect his little body this afternoon. The funeral will be on Friday. I will light a candle from you in church. Please come home to me soon. With love from Margaret.

Silence.

SHAW: Jack.

JACK: We should thank God. For his life.

SHAW: Aye. Aye.

JACK kneels. ARTHUR kneels beside him. JACK bows his head but cannot pray.

JACK breaks down. SHAW holds him.

TIPPER runs on.

TIPPER: Where's the chaplain? They said there'd be a chaplain.

SHAW: Not now, lad –

TIPPER: I haven't done this before. I don't know what to –

JACK: All right, Tipper.

TipPER: I shouldn't be here, Jack.

JACK: It's going to be all right. You heard the Colonel.

TIPPER: I lied about my age. I'm only fifteen. I didn't…

JACK: Here, son. Have a cigarette. Then we'll find the chaplain.

JACK gives TIPPER his last cigarette. STEPHEN appears.

The CHAPLAIN begins to sing: 'There is a Green Hill'.

STEPHEN: If you're there, Father…. Save us. Save my men… Save Isabelle.

ISABELLE appears.

STEPHEN: *(Urgently.)* Isabelle. I went to the cathedral –

LISETTE appears.

STEPHEN: I – are you well, Madame?

LISETTE: I hate you!

ISABELLE: Lisette!

61

LISETTE: I hate you both!

LISETTE runs off.

STEPHEN: She knows. She heard us.

ISABELLE: Oh God.

STEPHEN: I went to the cathedral. So many names, and only the blink of an eye till we join them. We have to leave, now.

ISABELLE: I –

The sound of the front door slamming. AZAIRE appears.

AZAIRE: Ah, there you are, my dear. Do you know, I just heard the strangest story… Apparently someone's been visiting one of the workers, taking him food…

STEPHEN: Yes, I heard that. A local man, I think.

AZAIRE: And the strangest thing was this woman was married to the factory owner. Isn't that odd?

ISABELLE: They were starving.

AZAIRE: … It's true.

ISABELLE: They cannot even feed their children on your miserly wage!

AZAIRE: … Leave the room, Monsieur.

ISABELLE: Let him stay.

AZAIRE: …

ISABELLE: Let him stay.

Silence.

AZAIRE: Bérard also said that you were, you were having a liaison. With one of the workers…?

ISABELLE: Not a worker… With Stephen.

AZAIRE: …

STEPHEN: It's my fault. I pursued your wife. You should blame me, not her.

AZAIRE: I don't… You can't…

ISABELLE: I'm so sorry.

AZAIRE: In my own house!

ISABELLE: René…

AZAIRE: Where? In your bed? In mine?

ISABELLE: It doesn't matter –

AZAIRE: It does to me! Which room?

STEPHEN: For God's sake!

AZAIRE: What will your father say? And Bérard… *(Distraught.)* What will they all say?

STEPHEN: What d'you expect, the way you treat her?

AZAIRE: What did you tell him?

STEPHEN: You think I can't hear? You're an animal.

They square up to each other.

AZAIRE: If you ever come back to Amiens, I will kill you.

LISETTE runs in, followed by GRÉGOIRE.

LISETTE: What's happening?

AZAIRE: You will leave at once.

STEPHEN: Of course. But I'm taking your wife with me.

AZAIRE: Don't be absurd.

LISETTE: Maman?

AZAIRE: Isabelle; you can't leave me.

STEPHEN: … Isabelle…

GRÉGOIRE: Maman!

AZAIRE: You're not leaving, you whore!

STEPHEN: How dare you?

AZAIRE: She's my wife!

ISABELLE: Stop it! Both of you!

MARGUERITE enters.

MARGUERITE: Excuse me. The children should not be –

63

LISETTE: Maman. Don't leave me.

ISABELLE: I am not a whore.

GRÉGOIRE: Maman.

MARGUERITE: Children, come with me.

MARGUERITE takes the children away.

AZAIRE: Forgive me. My love.

ISABELLE: I do forgive you. And I ask you to forgive me the wrong I have done you.

Beat.

STEPHEN: Isabelle…

STEPHEN holds out his hand.

AZAIRE: If you go with him, you're going to Hell!

A moment.

AZAIRE: To Hell!

The men come back on. ISABELLE and the memory disappear.

And we're in hell. The sound of artillery, building louder than ever. Shells whistling by overhead. The men terrified, flinching as each shell lands, while the men put up ladders, prepare.

Men gather by the CHAPLAIN.

SHAW: Jack… We should pray.

JACK: I can't.

SHAW: I'll stay w'yer.

JACK: You go. Say a prayer for me, eh? Say a prayer for all our boys.

SHAW goes to the CHAPLAIN.

STEPHEN looks at JACK.

STEPHEN: Firebrace.

JACK turns back.

STEPHEN: Did you get your leave?

JACK: No. Sir.

STEPHEN: After the attack.

JACK: Thank you, sir. Good luck.

STEPHEN watches the men, all bar JACK, going to the CHAPLAIN, kneeling to pray. The CHAPLAIN hands out the sacrament. A moment of quiet before the storm.

CHAPLAIN: In the name of the Father, and the Son, and the Holy Spirit.

GRAY appears.

GRAY: Wraysford.

STEPHEN: Wire cutters?

GRAY: … I'll recap the plan. The artillery lay down the barrage; you advance at walking pace –

STEPHEN: Walking pace?

GRAY: We have the Ulsters on one side of us and on the other, the 29th Division, fresh from Gallipoli –

STEPHEN: Fresh?

GRAY: For God's sake, man, I'm giving you our orders! The wire has not been cut. I've been up and down the line. Most of our shells have not gone off. Don't tell your men. Staff cock-up. Haig, Barclay, Rawlinson, the lot of them. They thought the bombardment would destroy it. Barely touched their defences.

STEPHEN: But that means…

GRAY: The attack will be in five hours, at seven thirty.

STEPHEN: We can't let this happen.

Pause. GRAY hands STEPHEN the wire cutters.

GRAY: I'll be with you.

STEPHEN: What should I tell my men?

GRAY rests his hand on STEPHEN's shoulder. They gaze at each other. Long pause.

GRAY: Don't tell them anything. Just pray for them, and write to anyone you love.

GRAY leaves. The sound of the shelling, louder and louder.
Silence falls.

EVANS begins to sing, his song continuing underneath the letter writing.

JACK: Dear Margaret. Thank you for telling me about our boy.

SHAW: Dear Annie. How are you, my love?

TIPPER: Dear Mum.

STEPHEN: Isabelle… I'm writing to you because we're about to attack.

JACK: I worry for you, Mags. What it must be like at home without him.

STEPHEN: I'm sending this to the house in Amiens because I didn't know where else to write. I don't know where you are, Isabelle. I don't even know if you are still alive.

JACK: We would've kept him but God knew best.

SHAW: Our boys are going over in t'morning. We'll blow our mines first, should see to it good and proper. They think there's going to be a big victory; can't be much longer now.

STEPHEN: I wanted to tell you what it feels like to be on the bank of the river again, fleas crawling against my flesh, and the lice – God, the lice –

JACK: God is merciful. He has given me back many memories I thought I'd lost.

TIPPER: Dear Mum.

STEPHEN: Just waiting. Some crime against nature is about to be committed. These boys are just grocers, clerks, fathers, sons. A country cannot bear to lose them.

JACK: I'll be home, soon as I can, to look after you.

TIPPER: *(Cries.)* Mum.

STEPHEN: Be with me. Help me to lead my men into whatever awaits us. If I survive this, let me find you again. Let me find you.

TIPPER: Dear Mum. Don't worry about me. When I was a little lad you was very good to me and I won't let you down. Write to me again. Please send me a couple of pictures of Upton Park. Your loving son, Michael.

SHAW: Cheerio, Arthur.

JACK: Your loving husband, Jack.

STEPHEN: I love you. I always will. Stephen.

EVANS finishes his song. JACK and SHAW leave.

STEPHEN hands TIPPER the wire cutters.

STEPHEN: Wire cutters, Tipper.

TIPPER: I thought the wire was cut by the bombardment?

STEPHEN: Just in case… You'd better get the others.

TIPPER leaves.

EVANS: Sir! D'you think I've got a minute to see my brother? He's only just signed up –

STEPHEN: I'm afraid there isn't time. I'm sure he'll be all right.

EVANS: Course he will. He's Welsh.

EVANS leaves. Infantry return, helmets on.

STEPHEN: Positions! Fix bayonets.

The infantry line up.

TIPPER appears without his helmet. Just a boy.

TIPPER: Any more rum going? Shit.

STEPHEN hands TIPPER his hipflask. TIPPER takes a swig. Hands it to the next man.

STEPHEN: Are you boys footballing men? Er…Tipper?

TIPPER: The 'ammers, sir.

STEPHEN: Then you'll like this. I heard the whole of the Hearts team are just down the line from us. Signed up together. Proving unbeatable.

TIPPER: Must make a nice change for 'em.

STEPHEN: We'll get a game going tonight, all right?

GRAY appears.

GRAY: Good luck, boys. I'll see you on the other side.

GRAY joins the men. Beat. BARCLAY too, with his sword.

STEPHEN: One more minute.

Silence.

STEPHEN: Wait for the whistle.

The sound of mines exploding. Smoke and dust fly up. Silence. STEPHEN looks at his watch.

STEPHEN: Not yet... Twenty seconds.

TIPPER takes out his German pistol. He raises it to his temple. He shoots himself. No one dares react.

STEPHEN: *(Voice cracking.)* Ten seconds.

The sound of skylarks.

STEPHEN blows his whistle. The men climb the ladders.

Deafening machine gunfire, louder and louder. There is no way through that wall of steel.

ACT TWO

SCENE ONE

Nearing the end of 1917. Amiens. A smoky bar, full of British soldiers.

JACK sings. Still trying. Just.

JACK: An old man gazed on a photograph in the locket he'd worn for years,

His nephew then asked him the reason why that picture had caused him tears;

Come, listen, he said, I will tell you, my lad, a story that's strange but true –

Your father and I at the school one /day…

ALL: Day / Met two little girls in blue.

STEPHEN WRAYSFORD enters. He goes to the BARMAN. The music continues underneath.

STEPHEN: Excuse me. I'm looking for the Azaire family.

BARMAN: Who?

STEPHEN: Madame Azaire? Isabelle.

The BARMAN shakes his head.

STEPHEN: They lived round the corner, in the Boulevard du Cange.

BARMAN: The road was hit.

STEPHEN: Yes, I saw. Is there anyone who might know where they are?

BARMAN: Everyone left… Or they died.

Beat.

STEPHEN: What about the students who used to come here?

BARMAN: Verdun.

Beat. The BARMAN pushes a drink to STEPHEN.

STEPHEN: No. I have to –

69

BARMAN: You are fighting for my country.

Beat. STEPHEN takes the drink.

ALL: *(Bar STEPHEN, sing.)*

Two little girls in blue, lad, two little girls in blue;
They were sisters, we were brothers, and learned to love the two;
And one little girl in blue, lad, who won your father's heart,
Became your mother; I married the other, but now we have drifted apart.

The men applaud. STEPHEN finishes his drink, ready to go.

A woman comes in. ISABELLE?

STEPHEN runs after her.

BARMAN: Hey!

STEPHEN hands his drink back.

STEPHEN: Isabelle! Wait!

The woman hurries off. STEPHEN catches up with the woman, puts his hand on her shoulder.

STEPHEN: Isabelle.

JEANNE turns around, shakes her head, turns to go.

STEPHEN: I'm sorry. I thought you were – Ma'amselle Jeanne! Do you remember me? Monsieur Wraysford. Your sister's –

JEANNE: I'm sorry.

JEANNE tries to leave again.

STEPHEN: I went to the house.

JEANNE: It was hit –

STEPHEN: Is she alive?

JEANNE: … Yes.

STEPHEN: You're here to visit her.

JEANNE: I live here now.

STEPHEN: With her?

Pause.

STEPHEN: Please. I just want to see her.

JEANNE: … It wouldn't be a good idea.

STEPHEN: How would you know?

JEANNE: She's not the same.

STEPHEN: None of us are.

JEANNE: I'm very sorry, Monsieur.

STEPHEN: Please – listen. You don't understand… Please. I fought, at the Somme. Will you just listen to me?

Beat.

STEPHEN: I don't know what she told you but – she ran away with me. We were happy. I thought we were happy. Then one day, I came back from work, and she'd gone. All her things, her clothes, just gone… She didn't even leave a note.

Beat.

STEPHEN: I swore, if I survived, I would find her… I had to lead them over. Tipper. He was just a child. And we just… walked out there. The Colonel, with his sword, didn't last a second… I turned sideways - to protect my eyes, I think - and behind me – men mown down, their arms flapping like, like dolls… I'm sorry –

JEANNE: Go on.

STEPHEN: There was a man, in a shellhole, begging for water. I got to him but his mouth was shot to pieces… I just poured the water into the hole in his face. I got to the wire. It hadn't been cut. Our men were running up and down, trying to get through. I went to help –

A gunshot.

JEANNE: You were hit.

STEPHEN: In the leg! I lay in a shellhole, I couldn't move, so I just watched… There was one of ours, he got to the wire but as he cut his way through, they got him. He hung on the wire. His boots were shaking as they filled him with bullets. They blew his legs off, slowly, bit by bit.

All day I watched the machine gunners pouring bullets into human bodies. At dusk, when the firing stopped at last there came this…this sound…from the wounded who lay there, but it seemed to come the earth itself. This…this moan…as though the soil…as though the whole world was crying out…

That night, the sappers came for us. There weren't enough stretcher bearers.

EVANS appears / stands.

STEPHEN: A sapper picked me up in his arms…but then he saw the boy hanging on the wire.

EVANS sinks to his knees.

STEPHEN: It was his brother. Evans took me to the aid post, and then he went back for his brother's broken corpse.

EVANS sings.

STEPHEN: All night he sang for his brother, whom he had carried back in his own hands.

Silence.

JEANNE: What happened to him?

EVANS disappears.

STEPHEN: They sent him home for a rest. Shell shock, they called it. He came back two days ago.

JEANNE: And you?

STEPHEN: Hospital, then they made me take some wretched staff job. I've been stuck in an office, looking at maps and lists, as we sent them out again at Messines Ridge, Passchendaele – more pointless…abattoirs.

JEANNE: Monsieur –

STEPHEN: I have to see her again. Do you understand?

JEANNE: … When I met you that time, you were so kind to me. I wish I could help you.

STEPHEN: Did you marry that man?

JEANNE: No.

Beat.

JEANNE: I'm thinking of you too. It wouldn't do you any good.

STEPHEN: I'm going back into the line. I just want to say goodbye to her.

Pause.

JEANNE: She was hurt, in the bombardment. She's not very strong.

STEPHEN: At least ask her – at least tell her I'm here.

JEANNE: … Come to the house, tomorrow night.

SCENE TWO

JACK and SHAW are curled up together.

JACK: Dear Margaret. Thank you for the parcel, which arrived safely. We're having a good time of it. Plenty of grub, lovely billets. Can't be much longer. Jack.

SHAW wakes, yawns loudly.

SHAW: You still not sleeping? I told you, you should wake me.

JACK: Then there's two of us done in. What good'd that do?

SHAW: I'll tell you what. I'll do your shift; you do t'next.

JACK: Don't be soft. Here, got a new one for you. There's this soldier, and he's sinking into the mud, up to his neck. True story, this. So I says to him, "don't worry mate, I'll dig you out." "Well you'd better dig fast," he says. "I'm riding an horse."

Beat.

SHAW: Reckon your jokes'd go down well at t'Palace. You should visit us, when we're back. Think you'd like Sheffield. Thirteen picture houses. Plenty of work, down t' mines.

JACK: I was thinking of moving. Start again.

SHAW: Aye.

Pause.

JACK: I can't remember his face well enough to draw.

SHAW: Jack…

JACK: I can't remember Margaret.

Beat.

SHAW: Draw me.

JACK: Arthur?

SHAW: You remember… You said….

JACK: Yes. Now?

SHAW: Yes.

JACK: I'm about to go down the tunnel.

SHAW: I've got this feeling –

JACK: Don't.

SHAW: Draw me. Jack. Draw me.

Pause.

JACK takes out his sketchpad. He starts to draw SHAW.

EVANS enters. He takes a moment. He gathers himself. Puts on a smile.

EVANS: Boys! On my way back here, I went to see that girl again, only she says she's not doing that sort of thing anymore! I told her that's not good enough; there's a bloody war on! Well, she says, if it's a matter of urgency, her mother would see to me. And you should have seen the bloody mother! Still, I don't like to disappoint a lady… But I've been pissing kittens ever since!

Beat. JACK and SHAW laugh.

EVANS: Best hurry up. The Captain thinks he's heard the Boche.

SHAW: Not again.

EVANS: Near our fighting tunnel. Well, let's get going Jackie-
boy.

SHAW: I'm doing it.

JACK: Arthur –

EVANS: One of you better get a bloody move on.

SHAW: I'm doing it. Jack'll do t'next.

SHAW turns to go.

JACK: Arthur… I…

SHAW: I know.

SHAW leaves with EVANS.

JACK continues to draw ARTHUR SHAW. Birdsong.

Focus shifts to STEPHEN, who stands waiting for JEANNE.

JEANNE: … Are you sure about this?

STEPHEN: Yes. Jeanne… Thank you.

*Focus switches back to JACK, who has almost finished his picture.
EVANS returns.*

JACK: Everything all right down there?

EVANS: Quiet as the ruddy morgue… What you drawing?

JACK: Nothing.

EVANS: Let me see.

JACK: Piss off, Evans –

EVANS: Don't be shy! Your mother wasn't.

*EVANS tries to take the notepad from JACK. JACK won't let go. A
slight tussle.*

JACK: Just piss off!

Silence. JACK looks at EVANS. His slumped, defeated shoulders.

JACK: You all right?

Beat.

EVANS: I've never done it.

JACK: Done what?

EVANS: You know. With a girl.

JACK: … What about the prostitute?

EVANS: … I couldn't…

   Beat.

EVANS: I just want to know what it's like, in case…

JACK: I'll take you along, son.

EVANS: What if my brother died, without ever having been touched by a woman?

   A sudden explosion.

   Pause.

EVANS: Arthur.

JACK: We have to bury him.

EVANS: You don't know he's –

JACK: We have to bring his body up, and bury him.

EVANS: It's too dangerous.

JACK: We'll timber our way.

EVANS: No, I meant the second explosion.

   JACK picks up his spade.

JACK: I'll do it then.

EVANS: Jack!

JACK: He's my best mate.

   JACK goes. Beat. EVANS picks up his spade, follows.

SCENE THREE

The Azaires' drawing room.

JEANNE reappears. She touches STEPHEN's arm gently.

JEANNE leaves. STEPHEN waits.

ISABELLE emerges, barely visible in the shadows.

ISABELLE: … Stephen.

STEPHEN: …

ISABELLE: How are you?

STEPHEN: …

ISABELLE: Would you like something to drink?

STEPHEN shakes his head.

ISABELLE: It was good of you to come.

STEPHEN: …

ISABELLE: Jeanne said you were wounded. Does it hurt?

STEPHEN is still unable to speak.

ISABELLE: I'm very glad that you're alive.

Pause.

Finally, STEPHEN manages words.

STEPHEN: What happened?

ISABELLE: The house was hit, two years ago. I was caught by some shrapnel.

STEPHEN: Let me see.

ISABELLE: …

STEPHEN: Let me see you.

ISABELLE slowly moves into the light. Her face is disfigured on one side, a scar running down from forehead to throat.

ISABELLE: It's so ugly.

STEPHEN: You're still beautiful.

ISABELLE: You don't have to…

STEPHEN: You're beautiful.

ISABELLE: … Stephen, listen –

STEPHEN: Is he here? Azaire?

ISABELLE: The town was occupied. When the Germans left, they demanded that ten hostages should be taken with them, back to Berlin. René was the first to volunteer. He wanted to do something good. From all this. But – [then]

STEPHEN: He's gone? Then we're - [free]

ISABELLE: No – Stephen, listen – The Germans took over the house. Some of them wanted me to… They were so unhappy. They were just boys. There was an officer who looked after us – after me. His name is Max. He stopped them. He took care of me.

STEPHEN: No –

ISABELLE: He's a good man. He loves me.

STEPHEN: A German.

ISABELLE: He's a man. Just flesh and blood.

STEPHEN: A Hun!

ISABELLE: He didn't choose to be born there.

STEPHEN: A fucking Hun!

ISABELLE: I looked for you, when the British troops came through town. I looked for you everywhere.

STEPHEN: Is he here?

ISABELLE: He's in Germany. He was wounded at, at the Somme.

STEPHEN: Jesus Christ.

ISABELLE: Stephen –

STEPHEN: I was there, Isabelle. I was there!

ISABELLE: I know… I got your letter.

STEPHEN: …

ISABELLE: I couldn't bear to think of you, trying to kill each other.

STEPHEN: A German?

ISABELLE: I'm leaving soon. I'm going to live with him.

STEPHEN: How could you?

ISABELLE: Please don't shout.

Silence. The sound of a child crying.

STEPHEN: What was that?

ISABELLE: I – er - It must be the little girl next door.

STEPHEN: Isabelle?

ISABELLE: I was just thinking about Grégoire. He's a soldier now. *(With forced cheerfulness.)* And Bérard has gone. He gave his house to the Commandant, so when the Germans withdrew –

STEPHEN: They'd never let you in.

ISABELLE: We're going through Switzerland.

STEPHEN: We?

ISABELLE: I – Jeanne was thinking of coming with me.

STEPHEN: The happy family.

ISABELLE: Don't be cruel.

STEPHEN: Cruel? You didn't even write a note!

ISABELLE: What could I have said?

STEPHEN: You could have told me where you were going. You could have told me if there was something wrong.

Silence.

STEPHEN: You loved me. I know you did.

ISABELLE: … Yes.

STEPHEN: Why did you leave?

ISABELLE: It was a long time ago.

STEPHEN: Please.

ISABELLE turns away from STEPHEN.

ISABELLE: … That morning, I –

ISABELLE's hands go to her stomach.

ISABELLE: I wanted to confess, so I went to the church. I sat in a pew for hours but I couldn't even bring myself to describe what we had done; in my husband's house! I thought, I thought we'd committed a crime against nature.

I knew I had to see Jeanne; I had to go back to my family.
I only meant to visit for a few days.

STEPHEN: And your father sent you back to Azaire.

ISABELLE: René begged me – and the children… I didn't have
any choice.

STEPHEN: You could have come back to me!

Pause.

STEPHEN: Jeanne could live with us too. We'll have a home, a
real home, anywhere you like –

ISABELLE: Max was badly wounded. I have to go to him.

STEPHEN: D'you love him? Do you really love this…
German?

ISABELLE: … Yes.

STEPHEN: The way you loved me?

Silence.

ISABELLE: Please… Go.

STEPHEN: You don't mean that.

ISABELLE: I had to let it go, Stephen. To survive. I had to let
you go.

Pause.

STEPHEN: Can I, can I touch you?

ISABELLE: Yes.

*STEPHEN goes to her. He touches her forehead, slowly runs his fingers
all the way down her scar.*

STEPHEN: I love you.

ISABELLE: I always will.

Pause.

ISABELLE: Go, Stephen…. Please. Go!

STEPHEN leaves.

ISABELLE collapses onto the chaise longue. She weeps.

JACK appears, filthy, by the body of ARTHUR SHAW. EVANS stands with him. They sing:

JACK / EVANS: *(Sing.)*
There is a green hill far away
Without a city wall
Where the dear Lord was crucified

JACK collapses, sobbing on the chest of ARTHUR SHAW.

EVANS: *(Sings.)* Who died to save us all.

SCENE FOUR

August 1918. The sound of shelling. In his quarters, STEPHEN reads a letter. JEANNE appears.

JEANNE: Monsieur. I am writing to tell you that Isabelle has gone. She left for Germany last month. I thought you would rather know. If you ever need a friend, you know where to find me. Jeanne.

STEPHEN screws up the letter, tosses it away. JEANNE disappears.

STEPHEN drinks.

GRAY appears.

GRAY: I think you've had enough.

STEPHEN: I told you, I don't want leave –

GRAY: I'm trying to help you.

STEPHEN: I don't want your help!

GRAY: Pull yourself together. For your men.

STEPHEN: What men? Of our battalion, 800 went over that day at the Somme. That night at roll call those present to answer their names numbered 153.

GRAY: If you falter now, you'll rob their lives of any meaning.

STEPHEN: Our lives lost meaning long ago. You know that. I looked into your eyes that morning. I saw the void in your soul, and you saw mine.

GRAY: … Those are intimate moments.

Pause.

GRAY: When the war's over and we put up our memorial, what will we write?

STEPHEN: …

GRAY: Ypres. Messines Ridge. The Somme, Passchendaele…. I hate their names. But there are four words they'll chisel beneath… "Final advance and pursuit." There must be one of those words you like.

STEPHEN: … Final.

GRAY: Good man.

STEPHEN: I have a friend in Amiens.

GRAY: Good. Go and visit him.

STEPHEN: Her.

GRAY: Even better. Go on leave, visit your lady-friend –

STEPHEN: She's not my –

GRAY: And then come back here, and we'll finish it off.

SCENE FIVE

Early evening. Amiens. The Azaires' drawing room. October 1918.

JEANNE: *(Coming in.)* She's gone, Monsieur.

STEPHEN: I know. I got your letter. I came to see you.

JEANNE: Would you like a drink?

STEPHEN: Thank you.

JEANNE pours him a drink. Hands it to STEPHEN.

Silence. STEPHEN drains his drink, re-fills his glass. He indicates papers JEANNE is holding.

STEPHEN: I've interrupted you.

JEANNE: I help to run the hospital. I trained as a nurse, when this all started. I thought I would hate it, all that blood, but it turns out I rather enjoy it. I just mean – being part of something bigger than myself.

STEPHEN: You look happy.

JEANNE: This war has set me free.

STEPHEN: You live here now.

JEANNE: I ran away, just as you said. I came to Amiens to look after – to look after Isabelle. I decided to stay, when she left.

STEPHEN: How is she?

JEANNE: They've settled in well.

STEPHEN: They?

Silence.

JEANNE: She told me you stared a lot.

Silence.

JEANNE: General Pétain says it will finish any day. Then you'll be free to resume your normal life.

STEPHEN: This morning, there was a boy lying with no legs where the men took their tea. I just stepped over him.

JEANNE: You're tired. But you can't give up. Not so near the end.

STEPHEN: I don't remember why we're fighting. I don't remember a normal life.

JEANNE: We're fighting for our countries. For peace. For God.

STEPHEN: Our countries? Is it worth dying for fields and hedges? And as for God…

JEANNE: You don't believe in God.

STEPHEN: I believe, I believe there is a room, perhaps just one quiet room…

EVANS appears, singing 'There is a Green Hill'.

STEPHEN: Where it is understood.

Ghosts from STEPHEN's past appear, join the singing: ISABELLE, TIPPER, BÉRARD, AZAIRE, LISETTE. MARGUERITE.

STEPHEN: All I can see, fields of ghosts.

JEANNE takes STEPHEN's glass from him.

JEANNE: Come with me.

Lights change. The ghosts disappear. The sound of a river; birdsong. The laughter of children.

JEANNE: Can you hear the birds?

STEPHEN: My men talk about skylarks. Even when we blow each other to bits, the birds keep on singing.

JEANNE: Perhaps they always will.

STEPHEN: Because they don't care. The birds, they're indifferent to human madness… Before this war, the world was getting better. For the last five hundred years or so. But if we were just leading up to this… And now we've seen what we really are. And that'll be the biggest problem when it's over. Not who wins or who survives. But what we do with this knowledge.

Pause.

JEANNE: What can you see?

STEPHEN: A boy, playing ball with his father.

JEANNE: You have to try.

STEPHEN: The sky. And the river…and fields… Golden fields…

JEANNE: What else?

STEPHEN: …

JEANNE: *(Gently.)* Don't you see? It's all one. The sky, and the river and the watergardens and you and… And perhaps, in your room, one day, it will be understood.

Beat.

JEANNE: You will keep trying.

STEPHEN: We will.

JEANNE: … Maybe we should run away. To Paris.

STEPHEN: I could set up your easel.

JEANNE: And I'll have a house, with a garden and a swing
for – and twice a year, we'll have parties, and there will be
dancing and –

STEPHEN: Not dancing.

JEANNE: All right, no dancing. But there'll be a band, and a
singer.

STEPHEN: Perhaps we could persuade –

STEPHEN / JEANNE: Bérard!

STEPHEN: Why are you so kind to me?

JEANNE: Oh Stephen…

STEPHEN: Your smile. It's extraordinary.

She holds her arms open to him.

He kneels at her feet.

She strokes his hair. He lays his cheek against her thigh. He sobs.

STEPHEN: Isabelle… Isabelle.

Pause. STEPHEN gets up.

JEANNE: Look after yourself, Monsieur.

JEANNE leaves.

SCENE SIX

November 1918.

GRAY: Welcome back. Now then, the sappers have dug above
the Boche tunnel. One of their men, er, Firebrace, I think,
has got the most remarkable hearing. Led us right to them.
He needs your boys to cover him while he lays his mine. If
we can destroy their tunnel system –

STEPHEN: I'll do it.

GRAY: Don't be ridiculous.

STEPHEN: Why should I value my life more than the life of a
simple footsoldier?

Beat.

GRAY: Come and visit me in Edinburgh. We'll have tea on the Royal Mile. Bring your lady-friend.

STEPHEN: She's not my…

GRAY: I'll see you on the other side.

SCENE SEVEN

Darkness – the tunnel. JACK and EVANS crawl in, followed by STEPHEN.

JACK: We're right above 'em now, sir. You wait here while I lay the fuse. If they break through –

STEPHEN: I'll kill them.

EVANS crawls to one side, followed by JACK.

STEPHEN: Is this blood?

EVANS: Yes. It leaks down from the shellholes. Fifty feet up! Still, best not to think about it… D'you want to play Fritz?

STEPHEN: If we must.

EVANS: I'd say he's got a younger brother, who only just signed up. His brother's a good kid, and he's handsome, and all the girls go crazy for him, which pisses off our man no end, but he loves him, more than his brother will ever know.

An explosion. JACK crawls in.

JACK: Right, we've got their tunnel. Let's [go] –

Another explosion. The lamp goes out.

STEPHEN: Hello…? Firebrace? Hello?

Silence.

STEPHEN: Hello? Hello?

JACK: Sir!

STEPHEN: What happened?

JACK: The Boche. Must've had our tunnel marked down. You have to get out. S'usually two explosions…

STEPHEN: What d'you mean?

JACK: They blow it in two places, to bring down the whole system. You have to get out of here now!

STEPHEN: What about you?

JACK: It's my legs. I can't feel 'em. I can't move. Sir, you have to get back – I'd understand.

STEPHEN: What about Evans?

JACK: Dead. They're all dead.

Beat.

STEPHEN: You got me out that time. I'll drag you back. Which way?

JACK: Back through the chamber, down the second tunnel.

STEPHEN drags JACK along. JACK cries out in pain but they keep going.

Another explosion. Earth falls to the other side of them.

STEPHEN: What does that mean?

JACK: There's no way back.

STEPHEN: But Gray will tell them we're here... They'll send a search party.

JACK: They'd have to blow it, risk bringing down the roof... They'll put us down as missing, say a prayer for us next Sunday. Can't blame 'em... We're trapped.

Silence.

JACK: I'm sorry, sir.

Long silence.

JACK: What's your name? I'm Jack.

STEPHEN: Stephen.

Silence.

JACK: Funny that it should be you, at the end.

STEPHEN: Why funny?

JACK: First time I set eyes on you, you was gonna court martial me.

87

Pause.

STEPHEN: Who would you choose to be with?

JACK: John. My son.

STEPHEN: How old is he?

JACK: He's... He'd be ten. What 'bout you?

STEPHEN: Isabelle.

JACK: Is she your daughter?

STEPHEN: A woman I loved.

JACK: Don't you have any children?

STEPHEN: No. Jeanne said we should have a garden with a swing...

JACK: Who's Jeanne?

STEPHEN: Isabelle's sister. She's got the most extraordinary smile. It starts with her lips; then her skin catches fire – not with blood like Isabelle, but with light... We have to get out of here.

JACK: I told you, we're trapped.

STEPHEN: What about that way?

JACK: Just the fighting tunnel. Dead end.

STEPHEN: We have to try.

STEPHEN goes.

JACK waits.

Music begins to play, in JACK's mind.

JACK: There ain't a single word for marriage... It's a sentence.

TIPPER appears.

JACK: Take Tipper here, take little Michael Tipper... No, he's gone.

The ghost of EVANS appears.

JACK: Evans here, he ain't fit to associate with pigs...

The ghost of ARTHUR SHAW appears.

JACK: The other day, I says to Arthur Shaw, I says... Arthur... Arthur...

JACK cannot go on.

STEPHEN crawls back in with sandbags. The ghosts disappear.

STEPHEN: Jack! I found boxes of ammonium nitrate! Behind a wall of these sandbags – here.

STEPHEN props JACK up with the sandbags.

JACK: An explosives chamber. How many boxes?

STEPHEN: I didn't count. Maybe two hundred? Could we blow ourselves out of here?

JACK: Mebbe. We're a long way down.

STEPHEN: But it could work?

JACK: Only use one box. You'd have to drag the rest hundred yards back. Take too long.

STEPHEN: Can't I just drag one box here?

JACK: Have to blow it in the chamber, or else... I'm sorry, mate.

STEPHEN: I have to try. Stay with me, Jack.

STEPHEN crawls away, to haul boxes back and forth.

JACK: *(Sings, breaking up.)*
Two little girls in blue, lad, two little girls in blue;
They were sisters, we were brothers, and learned to love the two;
And one little girl in blue, lad, who won your father's heart...

(Spoken.) John. John.

Music, as days pass.

STEPHEN crawls back in, exhausted. He collapses by the sleeping JACK.

STEPHEN: Just a few more boxes...

LISETTE appears.

LISETTE: Kiss me.

GRÉGOIRE appears.

GRÉGOIRE: Maman.

BÉRARD appears.

BÉRARD: I am very good at catching my prey.

LISETTE: I'll tell him. I'll tell my father.

AZAIRE appears, with his shotgun.

AZAIRE: I told you, I warned you you'd go straight to Hell!

AZAIRE loads his shotgun.

ISABELLE appears.

ISABELLE: I had to let it go, Stephen. To survive. I had to let you go.

MENDELSSOHN plays. LEVI appears. LEVI takes ISABELLE away from STEPHEN. ISABELLE and LEVI dance.

JEANNE appears.

JEANNE: Perhaps, in your room, one day, it will be understood.

STEPHEN reaches out to JEANNE. AZAIRE fires his gun.

The ghosts disappear. STEPHEN rouses himself. STEPHEN shakes JACK.

STEPHEN: Jack! Jack.

JACK groans.

STEPHEN: How do I lay a fuse?

JACK: Cut open a sandbag, empty it, fill it with powder from the box, lay a trail back to here.

STEPHEN: Stay with me.

STEPHEN crawls back, laying a fuse as he goes.

STEPHEN: I'm going to light it. All right?

STEPHEN strikes a match, lights the fuse. Silence.

The sound of an enormous explosion.

STEPHEN: Jack! It worked! They'll have to come for us now!

JACK: No.

STEPHEN: Why won't you live?

JACK: After what I've seen, I don't want to live anymore. The day you attacked on the Somme we watched, me 'n Arthur. The chaplain tore off his cross.

STEPHEN: This is man's doing, not God's.

JACK: They've all gone. Arthur... Evans... Adams, Wheeler, Cartwright, Turner. Little Michael Tipper. All them boys I used to dig the tube with. Got to Bank, 1912. We all signed up, every one of us. 'Cos the pay was better, you see. Just another tunnel. They never said we'd have to fight. The boys, they all used to complain about the food. I'd go along with it, but I never told 'em, it was better than wot I got at home –

STEPHEN: You love your son, don't you? Don't you want to see him again?

JACK: I just wanted to kiss him one last time. Touch his hair.

STEPHEN: You'll see him, Jack. We're going home.

JACK: John died, two years ago... Haven't prayed since then. Stupid. And Arthur –

STEPHEN: That's not stupid.

JACK: Twice in my life I loved more than my heart could bear.

JACK cries.

JACK: Never even got to say goodbye.

STEPHEN: You'll have more children.

JACK: Margaret can't.

STEPHEN: Then I will have a son... And, and I will call him John.

Silence.

STEPHEN: Jack!

JACK: ... Tell Arthur, tell him I...

JACK chokes again; he dies.

STEPHEN shakes JACK, violently.

STEPHEN: Jack…! Jack.

STEPHEN cradles JACK's body. LEVI crawls on. He has heard STEPHEN's cries.

LEVI: Hallo? Ist da jemand?

STEPHEN cries.

LEVI: Hallo? Ist da jemand?

STEPHEN: Hello? Is someone there? Hello!

LEVI: Hallo?

STEPHEN: Hello?

LEVI and STEPHEN dig towards each other. LEVI joins STEPHEN. LEVI holds up his lamp.

A moment.

LEVI holds up his revolver, cocks it, points it at Stephen.

STEPHEN takes out his knife, holds it up.

Pause.

STEPHEN drops his knife. He slowly opens his arms, spreads them out to LEVI.

LEVI drops his revolver, opens his arms to STEPHEN. They embrace; STEPHEN weeps.

STEPHEN: The war…?

LEVI: It is finished.

A moment.

LEVI: I want you to have this Star of David. It belonged to my brother.

LEVI gives STEPHEN his brother's Star of David.

STEPHEN: This was my grandfather's knife. It's all I have.

STEPHEN gives LEVI his knife.

LEVI: Never again.

STEPHEN offers his hand. Helps LEVI up.

Sound of skylarks; glorious light floods the stage.

STEPHEN: Dear Jeanne.

LEVI: Dear Mother.

STEPHEN: I do not know what I did to survive this.

LEVI: I do not understand what this war was for.

STEPHEN: German soldiers helped us to carry Jack's body up, into the light.

LEVI: Into the empty German trench.

STEPHEN: We dug a grave together, for Jack.

LEVI: We threw flowers on the grave.

STEPHEN: And then we shook hands.

LEVI: We promised to write. And now, now I am coming home.

STEPHEN: I climbed the ladder, over the top, one last time.
No hurricane of bullets, no tearing metal kiss.

JEANNE: Dear Stephen.
I am writing to you because there is something you should know.

STEPHEN: My body and my mind, tired beyond words,
But nothing could check the low exultation of my soul.

JEANNE: Isabelle made me promise not to tell you, but now she has passed away…
When she left you, all those years ago, she was carrying your child.

STEPHEN: I do not know what any of us did to tilt the world into this unnatural orbit.
I don't know if we can still call ourselves human.

GRAY appears.

GRAY: Come and visit me, son. We'll have tea on the Royal Mile.

JEANNE: Her name is Françoise.

> Come and find me, and you can meet your daughter.

STEPHEN: No child or future generation will know what this was like, will ever understand.

> Now it is over, we will go quietly among the living.
>
> We will talk and sleep and go about our business like human beings.
>
> We will seal what we have seen in the silence of our hearts,
>
> And no words will reach us.

The sound of birds singing.